Villa to Village

DUCKWORTH DEBATES IN ARCHAEOLOGY

Series editor: Richard Hodges

Also available

Villa to Village

The Transformation of the
Roman Countryside in Italy,
c. 400-1000

Riccardo Francovich
&
Richard Hodges

Duckworth

First published in 2003 by
Gerald Duckworth & Co. Ltd.
61 Frith Street, London W1D 3JL
Tel: 020 7434 4242
Fax: 020 7434 4420
inquiries@duckworth-publishers.co.uk
www.ducknet.co.uk

A catalogue record for this book is available
from the British Library

ISBN 0 7156 3192 6

Typeset by Ray Davies
Printed in Great Britain by
Biddles Ltd, *www.biddles.co.uk*

Contents

To Andrea Carandini and Chris Wickham

mentors in archaeology and history

Acknowledgments

This book has its origins in the Montarrenti project, an excavation of a hilltop village west of Siena, which we co-directed in 1982-87. The project began as a training venture for students of archaeology from our respective universities, Siena and Sheffield, generously funded by the Province of Siena. We were consciously following in the footsteps of Andrea Carandini's celebrated Anglo-Italian excavations of the senatorial villa at Settefinestre in southern Tuscany, while trying to examine historical questions about the origins of hilltop villages in Italy put to us by, among others, Chris Wickham. Apart from many reports and essays in *Archeologia Medievale*, the large excavations at Montarrenti are about to be published by Federico Cantini in a monograph entitled *Lo scavo archeologico del castello di Montarrenti (Siena). Per la storia della formazione del villaggio medievale in Toscana (secc. VII-XV)*. Completing this report has compelled us to revisit our thoughts on the formation of villages in Italy, and in particular, the transition from the Roman villa to the hilltop village. Of course we are drawing upon our experiences in Molise and Tuscany, and excavations such as San Vincenzo al Volturno, Poggibonsi, Rocca San Silvestro and Scarlino, where we owe a debt to legions of colleagues and students. In writing this book we owe particular thanks to Andrea Augenti, Will Bowden, Kim Bowes, Carlo Citter, Gian Pietro Brogiolo, Paolo Delogu, Karen Francis, Sauro Gelichi, John Moreland, Nicole Coolidge Rousmaniere

7

Acknowledgments

and Marco Valenti. Our special thanks to Chris Wickham who read and commented in his celebrated blue ink upon a draft of the manuscript.

Antella, Italy

List of Figures

List of Figures

1

The Debate

A village is different: to what? To the next village, where society has taken a different turn. Why? It is that 'why' that I do not wish to lose. I would wish to reduce history to its smallest elements, and see how each of them works and worked, these little bits that you can find at the back of any watch ...; but then I would wish to put them back together again. One can only do that structurally: the bits fit together in a structure. You can't just write the individual history of a thousand villages and towns and get a history of Tuscany: you have to see how the different but also similar, changing but also stable structural processes in each village contribute to useful generalisations about function and change, about values, about class, in Tuscany. And more: it's 'the way the machine works once it is set in motion', as Edward Thompson wrote about class: the watch, once it's put back, by now understood, has to be able to run again. So: I would look towards structural comparison of processes working dynamically, in every village, building up from the ground to a wider understanding. It seems to me that historical analysis is only meaningful, in a wider framework of understanding, if that comparative concern is maintained in view throughout. (Wickham 1995: 27-8)

Medieval villages and Roman villas appear to belong to two different epochs and two different academic disciplines, but are

11

these differences in large part the product of the division that separates archaeologists from historians, Romanists from Medievalists? Our aim in this book is to confront this divide in a study of an emblematic European region – Italy (Fig. 1). Our assertion, as archaeologists familiar with medieval villages, is that their origins lie in the transformation of the Roman landscape, and in the transition from Roman villa to Roman and post-Roman village. This book is a contribution to a lively

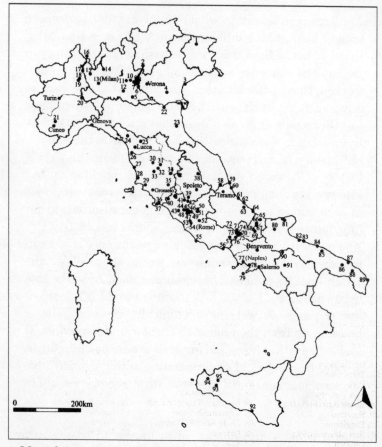

1. Map of sites mentioned in the text (see key opposite).

12

debate that involves archaeologists and historians of the ancient world and middle ages.

Two contrasting visions – one of continuity, the other of discontinuity and 'catastrophe' – have coloured our images of settlement and social organisation in central Italy in the period AD 400-900. On the side of continuity, the French historian Pierre Toubert, in his monumental work on early medieval Latium (1973), argued that the pattern of settlement remained (as it had been in the Roman period) essentially dispersed. He postulated an essential continuity in the landscape which was only broken, in the tenth and eleventh centuries, by the process of *incastellamento* (the formation of the fortified village). He interpreted the sites described in the written sources, *castra*, as the physical manifestation of that process. These new places, so Toubert argued, were not only centres of a newly nucleated

1. Ibligo-Invillino
2. Varone
3. Torcello
4. Monselice
5. Calvatone
6. Monzambano
7. Desenzano
8. Sirmione
9. Padenghe
10. Nuvoleto
11. Brescia
12. Pontevico
13. Milan
14. Monte Barro
15. Castelseprio
16. Muralto
17. Angera
18. Suzzano
19. Carpignano
20. Ticineto
21. Centallo
22. Ferrara
23. Russi
24. Gorfigliano
25. Terrazana
26. Pisa
27. San Vincenzino
28. Rocca San Silvestro
29. Scarlino
30. Poggibonsi
31. San Marcellino in Chianti
32. Siena
33. Montarrenti
34. Torrita di Siena
35. S. Salvatore (Monte Amiata)
36. Settefinestre
37. Cosa-Ansedonia
38. Nocera Umbra
39. Amelia
40. La Selvicciola
41. Bomarzo
42. Orte
43. Bieda
44. Sutri
45. Ponte Nepesino
46. Mazzano Romano
47. Mola di Monte Gelato
48. Castelaccio
49. Rignano Flaminio
50. Casale San Donato
51. Farfa
52. Tivoli
53. Capracorum
54. Rome
55. Anzio
56. Gaeta
57. Monte Cassino
58. Castel Trosino
59. Castrum Truentinum
60. Castrum Novum
61. Ostia Aterni (Pescara)
62. Ortona
63. Lanciano
64. Histonium
65. Vetrana
66. Guardialfieri
67. Santa Maria in Civita
68. Fagifulae (Montagano)
69. Matrice
70. Isernia
71. San Vicenzo al Volturno
72. Vacchareccia
73. Colli a Volturno
74. Colle Sant'Angelo
75. Colle Castellano
76. Venafrio
77. Naples
78. Oplontis
79. Villa Jovis, Capri
80. San Giusto
81. Avicenna
82. Barletta
83. Trani
84. Bari
85. Rutigliano-Purgatorio
86. San Miserino
87. Contrada Fontanelle
88. Santa Maria dell'Alto
89. Otranto
90. Melfi-Leonessa
91. San Giovanni di Ruoti
92. Eraclea Minoa
93. Entella
94. Segesta
95. Monreale

population, but also focal points for new forms of social control, new forms of production and distribution, and the framework for a new religious topography. For Toubert, the rupture which *incastellamento* created with the world of classical antiquity is epitomised by his belief that *castra* were almost always built on new sites, invariably located on hilltops.

Toubert's image of 'continuity' was constructed on the basis of his research on the texts from the Farfa archive, principally the *Regestum farfense* and *Liber largitorius*. For some archaeologists, however, the evidence from field survey and excavation told a very different story. In the early 1980s, partly in response to Toubert's model, Richard Hodges and David Whitehouse (1983) emphasised the fact that archaeological surveys of the Italian countryside consistently recorded a decline in the number of datable sites from the mid-imperial period onwards, and linked this to demographic collapse. Further, the general insecurity of the 'Dark Ages' is held to have driven the (few) remaining people to seek refuge in hilltop strongholds. In essence, Hodges and Whitehouse contended that the patterns of classical life came to an end in late antiquity itself. It is an argument that Bryan Ward-Perkins recently described as perhaps extreme and 'pessimistic' (1997).

In the twenty-five years or more since Toubert's monumental study has been in circulation, medieval archaeology has grown in Italy from a peripheral interest of historians to a major discipline, supported by numerous university departments. Not surprisingly, the archaeological evidence has grown exponentially, while our knowledge of the written sources has evolved only slowly in the aftermath of Toubert's paradigmatic intervention. Terms in the early and high medieval texts have been more clearly defined – such as *casale* or *villa*, often a group of dwellings, *curtis*, the centre of a manorial estate, and *castellum* or *castrum*, invariably a fortified centre maintained by a lord – while the process of *incastellamento*, the age of making *castella*

14

or *castra,* during the tenth and eleventh centuries, defined by the existence of foundation and other charters, continues to attract attention

Meanwhile, with minimum reference to the problems of site definition, major archaeological excavations undertaken with a maximum of stratigraphic control have provided the means to re-examine this debate between continuists and discontinuists. These excavations chart the transformation from dispersed classical settlement patterns, an archaeological phenomenon, to the agglomerated hilltop villages of the age of *incastellamento*, now both an archaeological and a historical phenomenon. Not surprisingly, the binary opposites of documentation for sites written in the past versus material remains obtained today, as well as continuity versus discontinuity, now appear to be little more than camouflage for a more serious dispute. This is between those who assert the primacy of the written word in the reconstruction of the past, and those who accept that material and visual cultural evidence constitute evidence no less significant than written texts.

A brief history of the debate

Romantic writers of the nineteenth century envisaged *castelli* as symbols of dark and barbaric times – in sharp contrast to classical antiquity. Later in the century, Italian historians such as Antonio Pertile and Francesco Schupfer were defining castles in terms of a social typology of the middle ages which distinguished between a feudal age, the age of the urban communes and the age of the principates based upon urban lords (Toubert 1995: 24). By the end of the nineteenth century, however, Ferdinando Gabotto and Gioacchino Volpe had identified *castra* as the bases of the rural aristocratic power that underpinned the birth of the communes between the tenth and twelfth centuries. At the beginning of the twentieth century,

Pietro Vaccari drew attention to the relationship between *castrum* and *territorium castri*: the *castrum* was the fortified village which grew from the *curtis*, leading to the establishment of pure feudal relations. Over the following fifty years several studies established the historical character of *castelli*, culminating in Mario del Treppo's essay on the *terra* of San Vincenzo al Volturno (1955) in which he identified the phenomenon as an innovation of the tenth century – an instrument not only of defence but also of control, created by a seigneurial class seeking to exploit their territories more effectively and re-populate deserted zones (Toubert 1995: 31-2).

The modern archaeology of Italian post-classical rural sites owes its origins to at least three different traditions dating from the early 1960s. Gian Piero Bognetti, a distinguished historian of medieval law, directed the first modern Italian investigations at the Lombard royal *castrum* of Castelseprio in 1962-3 in collaboration with a team of Polish archaeologists, while John Ward-Perkins, long-serving Director of the British School at Rome, sought to introduce the British methods used by the historian W.G. Hoskins and the Deserted Medieval Village Research Group in the late 1950s and early 1960s in South Etruria, and, concurrently, Joachim Werner, Professor of Archaeology at Munich, launched the excavations of the early medieval (Lombard) settlement at Ibligo-Invillino (Udine). Since these tentative beginnings forty years ago, literally hundreds, if not thousands, of sites have been either surveyed or excavated.

Each of these traditions possessed its own distinctive character. Bognetti was interested in the relationship between material culture and history. He was a proponent of the belief that historical knowledge determines how the archaeologist operates (cf. Wickham 1981: 3). The 1962-3 excavations at Castelseprio, near Milan, like the earlier excavations on the Venetian island of Torcello, were intended to reveal the material aspects of a Lombard settlement using stratigraphic methods. The excavation aimed to provide basic documentation from which wide-ranging historical facts might be reconstructed (cf. Delogu 1994: 240-50).

At the same time, under the overall direction of John Ward-Perkins, the survey of South Etruria initiated in 1955 was moving towards a new phase. Deeply influenced by W.G. Hoskins' seminal book, *The Making of the English Landscape* (1955), Ward-Perkins was keen to identify not only the prehistoric, Etruscan and classical phases of this changing landscape, but also the archaeology of the middle ages (cf. Ward-Perkins 1962; Wickham 2001: 38). To do this, ceramic remains from for the post-classical period were needed to identify medieval sites. The opportunity arose in the spring of 1960 during the survey of the Roman *Ager Veientanus*, some 17 km north of Rome. Deep ploughing turned up what on inspection proved to be the bases of a church colonnade, together with other major architectural elements and medieval pottery. Ward-Perkins soon identified the conspicuous surface remains as those of the *monasterium sancti Cornelii in Capracorio*, a monastery founded between 1026 and 1035 on the site of a papal estate established by Pope Hadrian I in *c.* 776 (Christie 1991). Ward-Perkins realised that the site had almost certainly been occupied by a Roman villa as well, and with some zeal set out to explore the possibility of establishing direct continuity between a Roman villa and a *domusculta* – a ninth-century papal farm. Over five seasons, under the direction of Barri Jones and then Charles Daniels, the British School at Rome uncovered this rare example of an early medieval rural settlement, permitting the pottery types of the age to be identified and used for locating other sites in the survey. Unfortunately, as Chris Wickham has recently written, 'Santa Cornelia did not have the impact of the Castelseprio or Torcello sites, or the German excavations of Invillino later in the decade, because it was not published for 30 years; by the time Neil Christie piloted it to publication in 1991, medieval archaeology had moved on' (Wickham 2001: 38). Wickham contends, though, that the most important outcome of this project was David Whitehouse's thesis and subsequent studies of medieval ceramics from Santa Cornelia and South Etruria. Along with John Hayes' seminal study, *Late Roman Pottery*, published in 1972 – 'one suddenly feels a breath of a different kind of air – scientific medieval archaeology, in English on Italy, begins here' (Wickham 2001: 39).

Joachim Werner's excavations of the fortified hilltop site of Ibligo-Invillino in Friuli were launched in 1962. Attracted by a reference to the site as a *castrum* in Paul the Deacon's eighth-century *History of the Lombards*, Werner and his pupils endeavoured to show how a late classical fortress served as an element of a Lombard *limes*. This in turn has led to a detailed discussion of the changing material values of this site during the Migration Period (Gelichi 1997: 132-4).

With this appreciation of the potential of post-classical or medieval archaeology for illuminating historical problems, many new projects were launched. It is pertinent to mention, first, Pierre Toubert at the École Française de Rome, who studied the Farfa charters, describing in some detail medieval settlement in the Sabine Hills west of Rome. Toubert's model, to which we have already alluded, has been the principal historical framework for research in this field since its publication in 1973. In essence, he showed that the tenth- to eleventh-century *castelli*, created during the age of *incastellamento*, for which there are plentiful written descriptions, owed little or nothing to the preceding settlement pattern. For Toubert, *incastellamento* marked a rupture with the past. Preceding *incastellamento*, according to Toubert, was a phase characterised by the *curtis*, in essence manors that in his opinion were largely isolated, dispersed settlements. The *curtis*, he contended, was introduced in this region in the ninth century;

before this, Toubert describes an aboriginal world in which the peasantry occupied dispersed households, or *casalia*. The origins of these households, although Toubert himself does not specify this, are commonly ascribed to the collapse of the classical settlement system in the sixth or seventh centuries. Toubert's model is fundamentally about the rise of local powers and their changing relations with the peasantry. In sum, a largely free, sub-Roman peasantry was effectively reformed with the introduction of a manorial system which Toubert thought evolved slowly in the region (unlike Andreolli and Montanari (1983), who contended that the manor was introduced following the Frankish invasion of the 770s). Toubert believed that this system was dramatically overhauled at the end of the millennium when the proliferation of local aristocracies gave rise to the need to control their human and landed resources more effectively in nucleated villages. With these new controls feudalism, so Toubert believed, had come of age.

In this context, mention should also be made of the 'leftist socio-economic history of Giovanni Tabacco's pupils in Turin (Beppe Sergi, Aldo Settia, Rinaldo Comba), who saw archaeology as the logical material counterpart to what they sought to do with documents' (Wickham 2001: 39). Further south, and much more topographically-orientated, mention must be made of (1) the enduring influence of the Florentine economic historian, Elio Conti, who looked at the agrarian structure of Tuscany, (2) the energetic work in Liguria of Tiziano Mannoni, a scientist at Genoa University, (3) the work of Paolo Delogu and Paolo Peduto at Salerno, and (4) the (British) Deserted Medieval Village Research Group, whose British and French adherents began excavating hilltop sites on a small scale in Latium, Basilicata, and Sicily.

As a result of these studies, when Toubert's monumental study of Latium was finally published in 1973, there existed a small body of sites which gave rise, for example, to an intense debate on *incastellamento* at the British School at Rome in 1975. Steadily, with the creation of the academic review *Archeologia Medievale,* and the making of university positions in medieval archaeology, the number of excavations steadily increased (Gelichi 1997: 84-7; cf. Wickham 1999). During the 1980s and 1990s, surveys of villages were published for parts of most regions in Italy, with large-scale projects illuminating the history and density of sites in the Abruzzo, Latium, Liguria, Lombardy and Tuscany.

Over the course of twenty years a fierce debate has emerged between archaeologists and historians. In the Cuneo conference of 1981 entitled 'Castelli. Storia e Archeologia' (Comba and Settia 1984), most historians keenly sustained Toubert's model of settlement discontinuity from late classical/early medieval dispersed sites and high medieval nucleated villages, although, tellingly, Toubert himself in his concluding address urged the archaeologists to develop a more ambitious form of *Siedlungs-archäologie* (1984: 407). Toubert, in effect, was recommending that German open-area excavations should be adopted in place of the modest trenching which had characterised most archaeological enquiry up to this time. To some extent, at places like Montarrenti in Tuscany, excavations took place on precisely the scale that Toubert had had in mind. Yet at the conference devoted to the results of Montarrenti excavations held in 1988, the historian, Paolo Delogu, while chairing a charged discussion between archaeologists and historians, seriously questioned the celebrated Toubert model and speculated that *incastellamento* in the tenth century was based upon settlement evolution over the preceding centuries (Delogu in Francovich & Milanese 1988: 267-75, esp. at 274).

Ten years later, with the publication of hilltop sites such as Montarrenti, Poggibonsi and Rocca San Silvestro in Tuscany (excavation sites which conform to what Toubert in 1981 described as *Siedlungsarchäologie*), it is now apparent that the archaeological evidence no longer affirms Toubert's interpretation based upon the written sources. As Chris Wickham, perhaps the historian who has made the most effort to use archaeological evidence, has recently stated: 'Rural economic history need not, and should not, be tied to the problematic of, say, the *"sistema curtense"* when so much can be said about the changing patterns of regional exchange and, increasingly, rural settlement hierarchies' (1999: 18).

The archaeological evidence challenges Toubert's notion of a sixth/seventh-century peasantry living in scattered, isolated farmsteads or in small hamlets, with the inception of villages coming much later, at the turn of the millennium. Instead, in many parts of Italy – as indeed in the Frankish territories – nucleated and dependent dispersed farmsteads of late antiquity moved to occupy new locations in the sixth or seventh century. The new settlements consisted of individual farms separated by fences, invariably located on hilltops. Moreover, the aristocratic estate centres or *curtes* that were once thought to have been isolated farmsteads are now believed to have existed right in the middle of pre-existing villages. The archaeology shows that the *curtis dominica*, the centre of the estate, was often simply a larger farmstead within the village. It seems beyond doubt that the estate system of the *villa rustica* – predominant in Roman times – was in the early middle ages replaced by a new basic unit of production, that is by peasant households cooperating as villages. Despite dozens of intensive field surveys in Italy, not a single case of continuity of a Roman estate (the farm and its managed landscape) into the early middle ages has been identified. Continuity, as far as we can see, has only been identified in the case of numerous late antique churches which were sustained, perhaps in episodic rebuildings, into the middle ages. We conclude, therefore, that the rupture attributed by Toubert to the decades around the year 1000 should be ascribed instead to the sixth or seventh century, when an extreme structural change of the economic system occurred. This model, based upon the archaeological evidence, has much in common with the circumstances in most parts of the old western Roman Empire.

'The village of the historians and the village of archaeologists'

The quotation comes from a review article by Elisabeth Zadora-Rio of Jean Chapelot and Robert Fossier's groundbreaking volume, *Le village et la maison au Moyen Age*, published in 1980 (Zadora-Rio 1995). Zadora-Rio's paper explains much about the debate between archaeologists and historians concerning the definition of the village, and as it is relevant not only to circumstances in France but also to those throughout Europe (cf. Ripoll & Arce 2000: 63-70), we will summarise its argument in this section, returning to it from time to time throughout the book.

In *Le village et la maison au Moyen Age* an archaeologist (Chapelot) and an historian (Fossier) established a model in which the birth of the village occurred around the turn of the millennium, with the nucleation of settlement located around fixed points. The fixed points around which villages formed were, according to Chapelot and Fossier, the church, its cemetery and the castle. Early medieval villages, as a result, were not considered to be villages in the medieval, legal sense. Fossier explained why in a later book: 'il leur manque l'essentiel de la fonction villageoise: un statut juridique, un rôle au centre d'un terroir, et surtout ce qui leur assure la durée, l'église, le cimetière, le château ...' (Fossier 1982: 191-2), lacking what Fossier described as the spirit of village life enshrined in relations both horizontally and vertically in legal terms. Instead, he defined early medieval settlements as 'un habitat', a more or less sedentary proto-village.

With many new excavations in France, Fossier's strict definition has been challenged. Settlements showing some semblance of organisation with small churches, cemeteries and evidence of collective artisanal operations belonging to the later Merovingian and Carolingian periods compelled the archaeologist Patrick Périn to contend 'that organised settlement, and at least the notion of the village, existed in France at least before the second half of the ninth century, and probably at least since the Merovingian epoch' (1992: 227). A year later, Jean Chapelot, perhaps in defence of his collaboration with Fossier, affirmed that in his opinion clear differences exist between early and high medieval villages: 'by contrast with the typical medieval village our rural *habitats* of the early middle ages show that a rupture intervened in almost every domain: generally, from the twelfth to thirteenth centuries, construction was made in resistant materials such as stone and, partially at least, this was the work of specialists like the tiler; there was a concentration of diverse functions in an agrarian unit in one or several buildings built in a permanent manner; there was a concentration of buildings in the space ...' (Chapelot 1993: 197). Zadora-Rio's article attempts to meet the problem of interpretation highlighted by Périn and Chapelot.

Fossier's interpretation of a village is one based upon the jurisdictional elements described in the written sources, particularly between the eleventh and thirteenth centuries. But, asks Zadora-Rio, how should an archaeologist, with very different source material, approach this problem? For the archaeologist, she says, a village is a group of houses. Like historians, archaeologists have not attempted to define a village as a particular number of dwellings. On the other hand, identifying the cemetery is, of course, straightforward for the archaeologist, whereas it is rarely described in the written sources. Likewise it is normally possible to identify a church and distinguish it, by the absence of domestic occupation, from other buildings, although without texts it is virtually impossible to distinguish between a parish church, a funerary chapel or a private chapel. Identifying fortifications is relatively straight-forward for the archaeologist. Only post-built palisades or earthen ramparts, later overlain (and therefore obliterated) by stone fortifications, tend to pose problems. Archaeology sheds light on production, distribution and, of course, consumption. The material culture ranging from coins and ceramics to faunal and botanical remains illuminate the economics of the settlement, from which archaeologists deduce the presence/absence of, for example, dedicated artisans and merchants. In the same way the existence of an administrative authority in a village is attested by the presence of a powerful agency reflected in the character of the defences and of the dwellings, the organisation of space in the village, and, of course, differential patterns of objects in dwellings and, where these occur, in cemeteries. Zadora-Rio cautions, however, that defining social hierarchy in villages is not always easy. Many of the dwellings excavated on eleventh- and twelfth-century earthen mottes in France are indistinguishable from those in their associated villages and, thus, without the raised earthwork the social distinction of the dwelling on the motte could not have been identified. More specifically, the archaeologist defines the nature of rural communities – an aspect that tends to capture the interest of historians who base themselves on the written sources – from a constellation of spatial characteristics of a settlement. In other words, the archaeologist focusses upon features such as the enclosure in which the settlement exists, the presence of a central place (such as a fortified residence, a larger dwelling or church), the regular elements of the plan, the presence of zones containing specialised activities, and the nature of the agrarian morphology (field systems, trackways, etc.) in the surrounding territory. Historians, of course, are cautious or even disbelieving of such criteria. Even when these criteria are satisfactorily applied to documented villages of the high middle ages, there is no reason, so the sceptical historian's argument goes, to believe

24

that the spatial characteristics of undocumented villages illuminate the nature of rural communities (cf. Toubert 1988 discussing the results of the excavations at Montarrenti in Tuscany). Zadora-Rio responds by pointing out that spatial hierarchies are clearly attested by the written sources in the early middle ages. She points to the existence of places described in the written sources as *vicaria, villa* and *colonia* and asserts that their relations surely illustrate some kind of site hierarchy that might be translated into the organisation of settlement. (In fact, as early as the fifth century, Augustine of Hippo was using the term *villa* to describe a village. For other examples see Ripoll & Arce 2000: 63-70.) Hence Zadora-Rio believes that we should reconsider Chapelot and Fossier's model, viewing the villages created in Merovingian times as precursors of the eleventh-century 'revolutionary' villages defined by Chapelot and Fossier. In particular, on the bases of their spatial characteristics, it is important to examine those elements which were sustained in the later medieval village and those which were not.

Notwithstanding Elisabeth Zadora-Rio's thoughtful reassessment of the situation in France, French historians working in Italy continue to be sceptical of the weight that can be placed on the archaeological evidence. For example, Étienne Hubert dismisses the evidence of post-holes cut into the rocky surfaces of Sabine hilltops as indicative of early medieval village life. He clearly subscribes to Fossier's distinction between habitat and village. The existence of wooden structures with a minimum of material culture, Hubert argues, is insufficient proof of village life (2000: 17; note also Toubert 1988 discussing the post-hole phases at Montarrenti in Tuscany); it was the progress from timber to stone buildings that transformed the countryside in an enduring manner (2000: 19). Consequently, Hubert questions the archaeological evidence from the one early medieval site recently excavated in the environs of Farfa, Casale San

Donato. Here, John Moreland discovered conclusive evidence of later seventh-, eighth- and ninth-century phases, contending that the absence of a ninth- to eleventh-century phase means that the *casale* of the early middle ages cannot be linked to the *castellum* of the age of *incastellamento* described in a document of 1046 (Hubert 2000: 11). (Another pupil of Toubert, Laurent Feller, has similarly questioned the ceramic evidence for the Abruzzo region where it seems to challenge the written sources: Feller 1998: 314; Staffa 2000: 63, n. 55.) Taking the opposite viewpoint, Riccardo Francovich and Maria Ginatempo argue that it is essential to take account of the early medieval archaeological evidence for hilltop settlements in order to understand the well documented process of *incastellamento* (2000: 14-15). Only by comprehending the passage from classical antiquity and the period preceding the documented phase of *incastellamento* will we come to comprehend the origins of local power, and, in particular, the evolution of all the elements, such as stone fortifications and dwellings, associated with the proliferation of local power from the later tenth century onwards.

Italy, late antiquity and feudalism: the aims of this book

Italy is often perceived in terms of classical antiquity – a country of fine, invariably ancient, towns set in flat, hot countryside. Nothing is further from the truth. The peninsula runs from the Alps to Sicily. Much of it is divided into three more or less equal ecological zones: first, narrow coastal strips either side of the peninsula, secondly, deep valleys and rolling hills, and, thirdly, a high mountain massif. This geography was conquered by the Romans, but from the fourth and fifth centuries AD there developed a profound regionalism that exists to this day. The Gothic wars of the sixth century, followed by the Lombard invasions later in the sixth and seventh centuries, followed in turn by Byzantine resistance in parts of seventh- and eighth-century Italy, followed by the Carolingian invasion of the peninsula in the later eighth century, must also be judged in the light of this geographical background (see Wickham 1981 for a detailed picture of the political history).

Much of the period covered by this book was determined not so much by migrations, as was once believed (cf. Härke 1997), as by tribal communities occupying niches in the landscape that either made ecological sense or were determined by some specific historical motive. Put another way: the age of the transformation of the Roman empire in Italy should perhaps be best seen in terms of returning to a world of competing territorial groups reminiscent of Iron Age times. Is it only a sense of the Roman unifying past, the existence of Byzantium and an awareness of Europe (La Rocca 1998) that distinguished this age from late prehistoric times?

This perspective serves to sharpen our historical lens. We need to reassess the validity of definitions as different as late antiquity and feudalism in the light of the availability of a new source material – archaeology. Late antiquity – the prolongation of the classical world into the sixth or seventh centuries – owes much to the celebrated Pirenne thesis (cf. Delogu 1998). 'The term "Late Antique" emphasizes the strong lines of continuity in patterns of government, in social structures, and in culture that tie this period to the preceding age of Imperial Rome' (Matthews 1993: 11). In a particularly illuminating essay, Bryan Ward-Perkins, while reflecting on the impact of A.H.M. Jones' massive survey of the later Roman empire, wrote as follows: 'More recent research, by both historians and archaeologists, has painted the period in much lighter tones, emphasising in particular dynamic change rather than suffocating rigidity. A generation of English-speaking historians, charmed by that wizard of words Peter Brown, has peopled the cities and villages of Late Antiquity, not with Jones's soldiers

27

and bureaucrats, but with saints and ascetics, and with their more fallible human followers. At the same time – but at quite the other end of the scholarly spectrum – the arrival in the Mediterranean of techniques of stratigraphic excavation, of systematic rural survey, and of detailed pottery analysis, brought about an archaeological revolution' (Ward-Perkins 2001: 167). Plainly, we must all begin to question whether this 'continuity' or 'elongation' is now justified, or , as Liebeschuetz has suggested, the product of a kind of contemporary political correctness resisting Edward Gibbon's view of decline and fall in the fourth century (cf. 2001).

This book opens up another historical hornets' nest: the issue of feudalism. In essence, the rise of feudalism in Italy, following in the footsteps of the classic French texts (cf. Carocci 1998; Wickham 2000), embraces a sequence of steps – first, *signoria domestica*, essentially a domestic mode of production; secondly, *signoria fondiaria*, a system involving those who owe limited obligations to the lord, but in which the lord does not possess complete hegemony over his community (Carocci 1998: 260); thirdly, *signoria territoriale*, where the lord has full jurisdictional power over the community in a classic feudal form. As Luigi Provero puts it: 'the centrality of the land in the socio-political dynamic is a common fact of all societies of the old regime, founded on an economy strongly agrarian in structure' (1998: 214). This is the context for the transformation of villages, by stages, into first the *curtis*, then the *castello*, to follow Toubert's typology described above. However, we must take a reflexive attitude to the tyranny of the term feudalism, as Elizabeth Brown warned us more than a quarter-century ago (1974). As we shall see, the archaeology of this age owes its roots to the fourth to seventh centuries: how, we must ask, does that affect the interpretation of feudalism?

It is perhaps fair to say that forty years after the landmark excavations of Santa Cornelia, twenty-five years since the publication of Pierre Toubert's seminal study of villages in Latium, and notwithstanding twenty years of intense archaeological study of the rural settlement in the first millennium AD throughout Italy, a charged debate persists about the transformation from villa to village. The debate can no longer be reduced to those who favour continuity and those who favour discontinuity. Rather, it exists between those who believe that the archaeological evidence provides texts that, in their own way, illuminate the written sources and reveal that the historical distinction separating the transformation of rural society in late antiquity and the age of *incastellamento* in the later tenth century is no longer tenable.

Put baldly, we are contesting the primacy of the written sources for this critical period. No one now doubts that when we find a textual mention, for example, of a *curtis* we think of a complex of a very complicated territorial form. We cannot, however, refer the toponym that localised it to a specific settlement or to a site. In the same way, when we come across documentary references to *mansi, sortes* and *case massaricie* (farmhouses) we cannot be certain that we are dealing with isolated settlements, since it is possible that other proprietors owned houses and lands in the same place without there being some form of surviving written record. In reality, often the only way of identifying a village beyond hypotheses about the names is by demonstrating, by means of painstaking linkage, that various mentions of farmhouses refer to one and the same place. Rarely, however, does the pre-1000 AD documentation permit such connections. Indeed, the sources are invariably too scarce for the construction of a stable glossary of the use of terms such as *locus, casale* and *vicus* (Ginatempo & Giorgi 2000: 174). In short, the documentation is at best sporadic, and principally offers qualitative clues. This is why we need measured archaeological data. For the archaeologist no such problems exist. A village from late antiquity onwards is a group of dwellings, occupied by peasants, aggregated within a defined space, which with time comprises further institutional components, such as structures indicating the presence of a local power in the settlement as well as the church. It is this definition, rather than the imprecise interpretation of the written sources, which permits us to create an unequivocal model of settlement evolution. Quite clearly, this archaeological model can be elaborated as a second step by cross-examining the evidence from the written sources. The early medieval scribe was almost certainly not interested in the problems we are debating here. His focus, understandably, was upon micro-historical matters, above all legal relationships. By contrast, our focus on the transformation of the Roman landscape necessarily demands a different order of information and a different perspective on the past.

The debate reviewed in this book pitches archaeologists against historians at one level, but at another attempts to move on from such binary opposites as continuity/discontinuity, dispersed/nucleated, and villa/village to re-examine the more complex picture now available to us. Further, the model advanced here seeks to assert that archaeology has helped us to rewrite a new history of rural society for peninsular Italy. In so doing, it sheds light upon the nature of the written sources and, incidentally, their interpretation over the past millennium.

The End of Villas and the Ancient World

Looking at the Late Antique world, we are caught between the regretful contemplation of ancient ruins, and the excited acclamation of new growth. (Brown 1971: 7)

Far from being a world from which all wealth and prosperity had drained into the hands of the few, leaving the mass of the population in a state of undifferentiated misery, archaeologists have revealed landscapes filled with thriving villages, dotted with comfortable and unpretentious farmhouses, in which the cities had changed their structures, but had by no means lost their vitality. It is a far more differentiated society than we had once thought. The time has come to pay attention to the intermediate classes who, in the present state of scholarship, exist in a 'grey zone' between the well-documented splendor and luxury of the rich and the dramatically depicted destitution of the poor. (Brown 2002: 48)

Introduction

The Roman villa constitutes a classic feature of the Roman countryside. Its origins in the Hellenistic world and dissemination to all parts of the Roman Empire have attracted an enormous number of studies. The demise of the villa, however, like the decline and fall of the Roman Empire itself, has generated many hypotheses. We must beware of generalisations, yet thanks to improved excavation techniques and a great number of field surveys in Italy, it is now possible to chart the transformation of the Roman villa as a rural settlement form.

Moses Finley contended that 'the Graeco-Roman world – was a world of cities. Even the agrarian population, always a majority, most often lived in communities of some kind, hamlets, villages, towns, not in isolated homesteads' (1977: 305). In Finley's mind, towns were the embodiment of civilisation and security as well as the arena for all important decisions taken in life. After all, the virtues of urbanism were extolled by contemporary writers, something reinforced in the decades before Finley was writing by the enduring achievements of classical archaeology. Since 1977, however, archaeology has laid bare the real character of the classical landscape. The density of Graeco-Roman rural settlement revealed by field surveys in the 1980s and 1990s was simply staggering. Paul Arthur calculated that 16,000 rural farms occupied the province of Caserta in northern Campania (Arthur 1988: 107). It is a figure that can be matched for countless other regions of the Italian peninsula. Finley's generation of ancient historians viewed the Roman countryside through the prism of their sources. Their sources, conscious of their audience, paid scant attention to Rome's people without history (to paraphrase the anthropologist, Eric Wolf (1982)) and instead lent emphasis to the grandeur of town living and country houses.

Roman villas, needless to say, were interpreted as monuments – rural reflections of urban living, as opposed to centres of estate management and foci in the ever-changing economic exploitation of a fertile countryside. So, for example, we think of a few grandiose villas – places that by the standards of other ages were virtually urban in character. First and foremost there is the Emperor Hadrian's great villa at Tivoli near Rome. Then there is the Villa Jovis on the island of Capri, a private retreat for the Emperor Tiberius. Other villas of similar scale include the Grotte di Catullo at Sirmione on a peninsula jutting into Lake Garda in north Italy and the well-preserved great house at Oplontis at Torre Annunziata, near Pompeii. Field surveys, of course, now show how exceptional these huge palaces were. Indeed, villas of this type are in fact rare in comparison with the thousands of small courtyard houses and the many thousands of simple farmhouses found in surveys and excavations in every part of Italy. Much has been written about these places and their role in the management of the early imperial economy and its dramatic transformation in the second century AD. Much too has depended upon a thesis that Italy exhausted its human resources during the second century and was unable to sustain such great places. The argument goes that the great crisis of such places was resolved by the introduction of smallholders to the Italian landscape who became increasingly tied by legislation. These, so the thesis maintains, were the forebears of medieval serfs (cf. Potter 1987: 99).

The archaeology is not quite as clear cut as some historians would suggest. On the one hand there was a hierarchy of country houses in the later Republican and early imperial period. At the apex of the hierarchy was the great house. Such places were undoubtedly rare. Excavations at Settefinestre in the later 1970s compellingly illustrated what they places looked like (Fig. 2). Settefinestre lay within the environs of the Tuscan port of Cosa. During the second century BC a small farm was founded on this well-placed terrace. A century or so later a great villa replaced it. The main residence of the *domus* was a perfect square measuring 150 Roman feet (44.35 m). The great house, with its slave quarters, was short-lived as it fell prey to the economic malaise of the later second century, and by the fifth century 'a small community of nomadic shepherds must have moved around with the homeless of the countryside after the

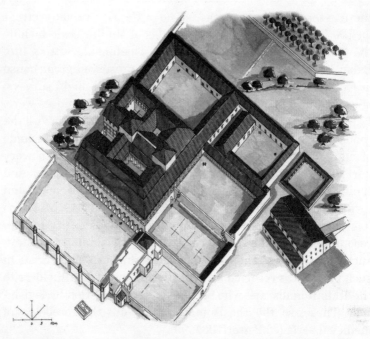

2. Reconstruction drawing of the senatorial villa at Settefinestre (Tuscany).

abandonment of the villa ... finding shelter and burying graves in the ruins of the settlement. To this miserable community it is possible to attribute ... some episodes of despoliation' (Carandini 1985: 91-2).

Next in the hierarchy were medium to small houses with accommodation for servants and slaves and accompanying buildings for accumulating the resources from their surrounding lands. The villa at Matrice in the Biferno valley is a good illustration (Fig. 3). Its origins lay in a Samnite dwelling that was enlarged over several centuries into a substantial property covering 2000 m². By contrast with Settefinestre, its architecture and internal decoration were austere. More than a day's

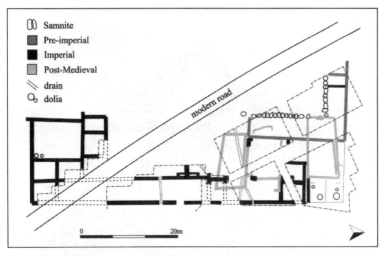

3. Plan of the *villa rustica* at Matrice (Molise).

journey by foot from the Adriatic coast, its economy was essentially derived from the valleys, hills and woods in which it was located. Such was the simple embedded nature of its economy, evidence was even found of a *glirarium* – a large container for fattening up dormice (Lloyd 1991: 237). As for its owners, the excavator postulated that they lived in the nearby small town of Fagifulae (modern Montagnano) in the Biferno valley, rather than on their estate. Occupation continued well into the fifth century, though the house shrunk in size before it was abandoned around AD 500.

Lower down the hierarchy were simple rectangular or square buildings – farms that accommodated smallholders, ranging from veterans to ex-slaves. Small agricultural villages – *vici* – also existed in many parts of Italy (cf. Patterson 1991). But as yet we know little about the character of these places, except their relative poverty in material terms. What is clear is that the great houses disappear in the second century, as do many of the medium-sized villas. Many, however, continued to operate on a more modest scale. The numbers of small farms declined too, but this class does continue. Hence Potter observed in the Faliscan area of South Etruria a drop of 20% in these sites in the second century, 40% more abandoned by AD 300, and within a century the figure of surviving sites is halved again. Notwithstanding some problems with Potter's data, it is generally agreed that there was a gradual and far-reaching transformation of the rural landscape (Potter 1979).

A brief survey of villa decline

The survey archaeologist certainly needs a good pair of boots, and a thick skull also undoubtedly helps, but most of all you need a broad back capable of warding off not just the dogs and slingstones of angry farmers but the scholars of posterity too. (Barker 1991: 7)

Scholars have now generally accepted that the Roman landscape, or more accurately, landscapes, disintegrated at a certain point. Research carried out throughout Italy, from Lombardy to Sicily, has revealed certain common features consistent with changes that encompassed much of the later empire (cf. Ripoll & Arce 2000). First, the system of slave villas existed only on the Tyrrhenian coast in central Italy, while it was absent in the Po region, and in the mountainous Apennine regions it co-existed with other forms of settlement. Secondly, the third-century economic decline affected all the Italian regions: it was strongest where the villa system was most structured and less drastic in the areas where the villa co-existed with pre-Roman systems centred on, for example, the village (*vicus*) or small-scale dispersed settlement. Nevertheless, this first selection process did not determine radical changes in the economic and settlement structures in the countryside. Thirdly, a partial revival occurred during the age of the Emperor Constantine in the fourth cen-

2. The End of Villas and the Ancient World

tury. The re-planning of the layout of many villas (cf. Ellis 1988; 1993), from the Val d'Arno in Tuscany to the Po regions, is one apparent feature of the Constantinian era. The redistribution of residential space, well illustrated in the villa at San Giovanni di Ruoti (Basilicata), for example, was, in fact, part of a more general process of transformation (see below). This transformation not only encompassed all aspects of the living arrangements of villas (cf. Ellis 1993), but also the management and use of their lands, with a steady return to mixed agrarian regimes in vast areas that had previously, at the height of the early empire, been used for specialised farming. A final common element is the slow decline that between the beginning of the fifth and the end of the sixth century led to the end of the villa as a settlement type. This was caused by changing social and economic circumstances, as we shall see, but also by lesser issues such as obtaining building materials to maintain existing properties.

Each villa excavated in Italy, from that in Contrada Fontanelle (Calabria) to the one in the Avicenna area at Piano di Regionali Carpino (Puglia), to La Selvicciola (Lazio), to San Vicenzino (Tuscany), and to Russi (Romagna), has shown that there was a considerable reduction of the inhabited area with the subdivision of rooms, the presence of earthen floors as opposed to mosaics, and, invariably, the insertion of wooden huts over earlier mosaic pavements. Cemeteries were commonly established both inside and outside the perimeters of the buildings, as inside the decaying remains of Settefinestre (see above) or, for example, San Vincenzo al Volturno, an estate centre in Molise. Simple stone buildings, perhaps makeshift shelters, point to a sometimes temporary occupation of ruins. Rubbish, too, now piled up inside occupied buildings as at San Giovanni di Ruoti (Basilicata), and around the tower of the estate centre at San Vincenzo al Volturno (Molise). In fact, most of the villas active in the second century were, like Matrice in

Molise (see above), dilapidated complexes by the fifth and sixth centuries.

Generalisations of this kind inevitably level out any regional features on which it would be interesting to focus, even in a short survey like this. In some areas, for instance, signs of decline already existed in the third century; in others decline occurred only as late as the fourth century. Although the crisis led to desertion and deterioration, it was lessened by an expansion of the population into new areas and even by significant changes in agrarian production. In northern Italy, the transformation started in the third century. Studies carried out in the Trentino valley, in the area around Lake Garda near Verona, and in the region of Emilia, have shown that villas and farms were deserted or underwent severe structural deterioration, and the countryside showed clear signs of similar abandonment (Brogiolo 1996a). An initial phase of decline was followed by a partial recovery that lasted until the Theodosian age, sometimes leading to expansion towards previously uncultivated areas. The reasons for this process may be traced back in particular to a renewed link with urban centres. For example, Milan's status as the imperial capital during the period AD 286-402 may have affected the area between Lombardy and the Trentino. However, in marked contrast to Rome's relationship with its hinterland, the impact of Milan's newly-won standing on the re-organisation of its countryside is as yet unknown.

The excavation of some Lombard settlements, such as Angera, Calvatone and Muralto, has revealed how smaller settlements played a mediating role between the cities and the countryside in the later Roman period. Here, excavated data show that the third-century decline had little substantive effect, and indeed a certain prosperity developed during the fourth century. If such intermediary centres in the distribution chain of goods were hardly affected by the first wave of recession, this means that the greatest repercussions were felt by weaker places at the bottom of the settlement hierarchy. Of the 70 known sites in Lombardy (50 villas and 20 rural buildings), 10 expanded during the fourth and fifth centuries with the addition of important and sometimes monumental transformations: the villas at Sirmione, Padenghe and Monzambano were reconfigured in the fourth century, and Sirmione (once again) and Desenzano in the fifth. The early imperial *mansio* at Trino on the road between Milan and Pavia was reoccupied in the later fourth and fifth centuries; later still part of it was transformed into a church which served as a nodal point in a later medieval village (Negro Ponzi Mancini 1999). Around the prosperous towns of Brescia and Verona during the fourth and fifth centuries, as Gian-Pietro Brogiolo has tellingly shown, the inhabited areas and the intensive cultivation of the land were converted into a complex network of villas, farms and simple houses (Brogiolo 1996b).

Further to the north-east, from the fourth century, the trend towards partial demographic growth and the farming of new lands affected the Trentino region where new dwellings were built in the hilly areas. It remains unclear whether the inhabitants shifted up to occupy higher land because of some instability, or whether they were seeking attractive, new areas to cultivate. Nevertheless, the continuity of some burial-grounds linked to the various *fundi* shows that this process did not involve the total desertion of the older, established classical countryside.

Further south, Tuscany, and in particular the coastal region around Grosseto, has witnessed sufficient research and excavations to permit hypotheses about the complex pattern of transformation. In this area, the absence of a polarising urban centre and the progressive decline of many smaller centres of the early imperial period make it difficult to establish the relationship between city and the countryside. Moreover, the third/fourth-century crisis did not lead to a generalised shift of cultivated areas to previously peripheral zones, but rather permitted the survival of a certain number of more efficient farmsteads as was shown in the *Ager Cosanus* – the Albegna valley survey close to ancient Cosa (Fentress and Perkins 1989; Regoli in Carandini and Cambi 2002: 218-27). The transformation processes of the countryside led to the success of (private and public) estates founded upon certain ancient, even maritime, villas, or on villages. The re-emergence of the village as a focus of aggregation is a feature that is found in quite different and widely separated areas. However, the question arises as to what degree villas had already become small villages in this period. Indeed, there is evidence of the transformation of several *mansiones* along the consular roads, *thermae*, and sentry posts into villages. On the Tuscan coast, the maritime villas that cultivated the fishing resources of the lagoons and ponds still played an important role, bucking the trend of decline. However, during the fifth century even these places underwent profound changes, becoming smaller and internally reorganised, as if to suggest that production on their estates was also being reorganised (Valenti 1996b).

Central Tuscany experienced a similar decline in the number of sites with respect to the early empire (up to 90% of sites disappeared). However, around the Roman centre of Siena settlement patterns based on medium-large farmsteads seem to have prospered. In the more distant hills south of Siena (such as Valle dell'Ombrone and Val d'Orcia on the north-east slopes of Monte Amiata), estates at the centre of medium-sized properties, appear to have been divided up into farmsteads, suggesting a system of surplus farming destined for the city.

To complete the picture of Tuscany, brief mention must be made of the northern part of the region around Lucca and the *Ager Pisanus* in which Pisa was located. Here the fourth-century revival was the result of the combined presence of a number of villas set out on a wide grid as well as family-run agricultural and pastoral farming that also made use of the Apennine woods for lumber production.

Proceeding southwards, a similarly varied picture appears to exist. On the northernmost edge of the region of Latium, decline was already underway in the Monti della Tolfa by the third century. However, much as in parts of neighbouring Tuscany, there were signs of recovery in the hill settlements from the fourth century that continued until the Gothic war. Further south, in the heartlands of the Campagna Romana, the hinterland of the metropolis of Rome, the medium-sized villa of Mola di Monte Gelato excavated by Tim Potter was deserted in the third century and re-occupied between the fourth and sixth centuries. Careful investigation showed a re-planning of the ancient structures, and subdivision of rooms and their functions, following a pattern we have already seen (Potter & King 1997; see Chapter 4). Potter's discoveries provide a model for other sites known only from small-scale investigations or from the celebrated South Etruria survey initiated by John Ward-Perkins (see Chapter 1).

The number and quality of studies in other contexts, such as the regions of Abruzzo, Apulia, and Sicily, may better illustrate the various specific factors in the dramatic dissolution of ancient landscapes. Inland, along the Apennines, the village had remained the main settlement pattern throughout the Roman period. In the Abruzzo, the third- to fourth-century decline left the territorial organisation of late antiquity virtually intact at least until the Gothic war occurred in the sixth century. Continuity has been noted by Andrea Staffa not only in the large coastal valleys (along the Vomano, the low Teramo valley, the Salinello and Vibrata valleys and the lower Pescara valley), but also in numerous small villages (2000). Further south, in the Biferno valley in Molise, the period of late antiquity was characterised by a halving of the number of sites, with clear signs of functional modifications (Lloyd 1995). Smaller localities, espe-

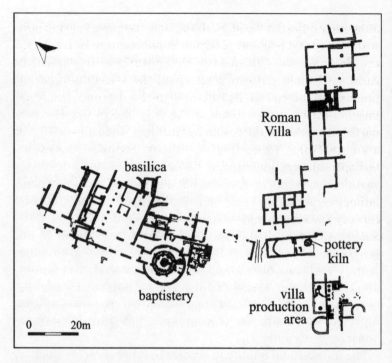

Roman
Villa

basilica

pottery
kiln

baptistery

villa
production
area

0   20m

4. Plan of the imperial estate at San Giusto (Apulia) (after Giuliano Volpe).

cially those inland from the Adriatic sea and closest to the Matese mountains, were worst hit by the crisis; larger complexes (such as the villa excavated by John Lloyd at Matrice, midway up the valley) managed to survive until well into the fifth century (Lloyd 1995). In the neighbouring Volturno valley, set in the centre of the peninsula, most villas and small sites disappeared after the third-century crisis, though a new estate centre and perhaps an accompanying village took shape at San Vincenzo al Volturno around AD 400 and prospered well into the sixth century (Hodges 1997).

The regions of Apulia and Sicily seem to have experienced an altogether different trend. Both regions, of course, boasted ports with strong and resilient maritime connections to North Africa, the Balkans, and the eastern Mediterranean. In Apulia the rural settlement pattern determined the selection of certain production centres that prospered to the detriment (and demise) of others. Excavations at the villa of San Giusto in the northern reaches of the region by Giuliano Volpe illustrate such a centre (Volpe 1998) (Fig. 4). Almost certainly this was a bishop's seat on an imperial *fiscus* which not only attracted sustained agrarian investment but also a growing level of population (see below). In Sicily, on the other hand, in about the fifth century, the rural population was still concentrated in localities long since established in the earlier Roman age (medium and large villas as well as *vici*). Because in some cases tenth-century pottery has been discovered on Roman sites, both in surveys and selective excavations, the question has arisen as to whether there was continuous occupation from the Byzantine period until the ninth-century Arab invasion and beyond (Molinari 1994).

Let us now look in more detail at three different examples of sites, already mentioned above.

San Giusto – an imperial estate and bishopric?

Towards the north of the dry, rolling Tavoliere Plain, some 50 km inland from the Adriatic Sea, the villa at San Giusto was discovered in 1985 when a plan to build a dam in the area was under discussion. Large-scale excavations by Giuliano Volpe in 1995-97 brought to light an important sequence of remains throwing interesting light on an exceptional villa (Fig. 4).

San Giusto started life as a late Republican *villa rustica*. The first major villa dates to the first to second centuries, but its zenith belongs to the fourth to sixth centuries. The early imperial villa comprised two parts: a residential building and an associated building that was used later for wine production. The residential building boasted fine mosaics, and was significantly enlarged and refurbished in the fourth century. The excavator believes that San Giusto may well have been part of a large imperial *latifundium* – a *saltus* – one of several imperial properties in this part of Apulia. However, from the fifth century, Volpe believes, San Giusto had an added role. In phase IIIA, the mid-fifth century, the associated production sector was expanded and, in addition, a large aisled church was constructed at the site with a notable baptistery. The excavator believes that San Giusto had become the seat of a bishopric and associates the site with Bishop Probo, mentioned together with Giusto, Bishop of Larino, in a letter of Gelasius I (493-4) and with *Probus episcopus Carmeianensis* who was present at a synod in 501-4. Volpe identifies one of the rooms attached to the church as a *gazophylacium* – where the offerings of the faithful were kept – on the basis of a hoard of over a thousand coins found here. The latest coin, minted between 523 and 530, provides a date for the cataclysmic fire which destroyed the church. Volpe ascribes this to a mid-sixth-century sack during the war between the Byzantines and Goths. Following this a new church (church B) was constructed alongside the ruins of the earlier basilica, much of which was dedicated to graves. The continued use of church B into the seventh century makes one ask about the gradual abandonment of the site. Was there a shift from wine production – so evident in the use of vats in earlier periods – to mixed farming with an emphasis upon cereals? Was there a change in the nature of the community? Either way, apparently much of the remainder of the site fell into abandonment, although traces were found of makeshift occupation by post-built structures.

This complex, well-stratified villa provides important insights into the period. Here is an example of a major estate in later Roman times. Quite clearly it is modest in scale by comparison with the senatorial villa at Settefinestre, and, but for its mosaic pavements, has more in common with the upland complex at Matrice. That is, with one exception. The two churches and associated baptistery reveal the new indices of the age: metropolitan standards imposed in the countryside. In its fifth-century heyday the complex as a whole was growing in size and rich in material culture. However, falling victim to the Gothic wars, its recovery is again illuminating: the church was still significant, but the nucleus of makeshift buildings and post-built structures is a harbinger of a new age. San Giusto appears to have been reduced to a church and a village sustained on a mixed agricultural regime as opposed to the highly specialised wine-production that had been so important for much of its long history.

San Giovanni di Ruoti: a classic late Roman villa?

Set in the rolling hills of Basilicata – a land that in recent times has experienced the gravest poverty – the excavations of San Giovanni di Ruoti have brought to light an important example of a Roman villa which, in a markedly transformed arrangement, existed until the sixth century (Fig. 5). The villa owed its origins to the early Roman period, when like other medium-sized estate-centres in this part of Basilicata, it exploited mixed economic agrarian opportunities, ranging from polyculture to pastoralism. The early villa, however, was rebuilt twice before it was largely abandoned after the second- to third-century crisis. Then parts of it were reoccupied in the later fourth to sixth centuries.

Only rooms 5, 7 and 8 survived from the earlier to the later rebuild in the fifth century. Room 5 was modified to be round and roofed with a dome. A close parallel at Centcelles in Spain suggests that it was designed as a tomb, but since there is no trace of burial its function remains unknown. Of the totally new structures, room 14 was a small tower. Room 15, which had a mosaic floor, and rooms 11 and 13 together formed a separate apartment on the ground floor. Rooms 9, 12, 10 and 39 were the cellars of an apsidal hall on an upper floor, which was approached by a staircase. Rooms 2 and 3 were probably a stable. The pottery indicates a date *c*. 460 for the new construction and *c*. 530 for its destruction (Small & Buck 1994).

The excavators suggest that the new villa was the home of a *dominus* living in 'Gothic style' with a first floor hall (cf. Potter 1987: 213-14). On the other hand the simple, geometric mosaic belonging to this phase of the house is 'something distinctively local' … the product of 'a workshop which retains some of the old fashions, though its repertory of traditional motifs is running low, but which is also capable of adopting and absorbing new elements and new styles from outside' (Dunbabin 1983: 57).

In the final report the excavators speculate as follows:

It is also possible that the plan of the villa points to new occupants with some un-Roman social customs. The clearest sign is the way they disposed of their garbage. The inhabitants of the previous villas followed the normal Roman practice of removing refuse from their buildings; but the occupants of the late villa at San Giovanni dumped their kitchen waste in the corridors and empty rooms, and immediately outside the entrances to the site. Most of the midden piles date to the last part of the fifth century and to the beginning of the sixth, and belong to the second phase of this villa, but some go back to the beginning of its first phase, *c*. AD 400. Even the dining customs may have changed, for if the long narrow room with a mosaic floor at the northeast end of the site is a dining room, as seems likely, then the inhabitants must have eaten there seated beside a long table, as was the practice of Germanic barbarians, rather than reclining around a low table in

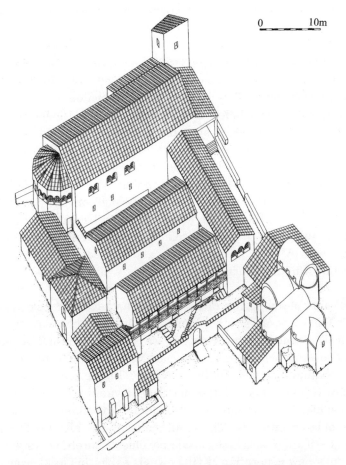

0   10m

5. Reconstruction of San Giovanni di Ruoti (Basilicata).

traditional Roman fashion, for there is no room there for a *stibadium*. A few artifacts of Germanic type add to the impression that the inhabitants of the latest villa were of Germanic rather than Roman stock. If so, they may have settled at San Giovanni as early as the beginning of the fifth century. (Small & Buck 1994: 4-5)

Notwithstanding this interpretation as one of ethnic transformation, the excavators note that

> by comparison with the first two villas, the latest villa was
> a relatively prosperous place. There can be no doubt that
> its prosperity was derived from pork production. Lucania
> was already famous for its pork before Roman times, but
> swine-raising became especially important there in the
> late empire when pork was levied from South Italian
> communities to provision Rome. By the middle of the fifth
> century the tax in live pigs was commuted for gold, which
> was used by the swineherds to buy pigs on the local
> markets .... Although the dominus of San Giovanni may
> have sold pigs to swineherds in return for gold, it is
> noteworthy that no gold coins and indeed coins were
> found. (Small & Buck 1994: 5)

Gold coins, of course, are rarely found in archaeological excavations. Pig bones, on the other hand, are common. The excavators'
analysis is thought-provoking. Are we really to believe that the
San Giovanni pigs were herded more than 500 km to Rome by
the servants of a new Gothic *dominus*? Taking our survey of
Italian villas into account, is not San Giovanni a classic illustration of a new community responding to the changing conditions of later antiquity? The small compact villa, albeit with its
unusual if unexceptional mosaic pavement, surely bears wit-
ness to a new generation of villa owners exploiting local econo-
mies. Does their attitude to dining and cleanliness make them
Romans or barbarians? Certainly there were changing cultural
mores. But are these not illustrative of new rural centres as far
north as Lake Garda where an agrarian hierarchy, in imitation
of urban form, adopted a new fashion of dining, and as in towns,
had new attitudes to refuse? Returning to the pigs, is it not more
likely that these fast-food products were managed locally to

sustain a weak but nevertheless embedded economic regime? Such places, it is tempting to conclude, after the survey of Italy, were exceptions, not the rule. The rule, it seems probable, is manifested at San Giovanni once the complex has fallen into disrepair, and refuse builds up in some rooms while others are left unroofed, and, in a telltale sign, an oven is built into a doorway, blocking access to the room behind it. Herein are rural inhabitants with cultural values different to those espoused by the *dominus* (with his metropolitan values) who had commissioned the mosaic, and similar in many respects to the last (fifth-century) occupants of the senatorial villa at Settefinestre, cast as elegaic shepherds by the excavator – in reality a new class of rural peasantry (cf. Carandini 1985: 91-2).

Torrita di Siena – from villa to village

Situated south of Siena, in the rolling hills of central Tuscany, Torrita di Siena was initially a late Republican villa (Fig. 6). The first villa comprised three colonnaded ranges set around a courtyard. In the first century AD the building was restructured with the addition of stables and stores as well as accommodation and bathing facilities that have lead the excavators to interpret it as a *mansio* on the Via Cassia. Close by a line of small buildings were constructed during the first century. One of these was probably a forge. The *mansio* was abandoned in the second century, and it seems likely that the small associated structures were either deserted or occupied only episodically over the following century or so. Reoccupation of the site occurred in the fifth century. Only part of the ruined *mansio* was used, while many parts of it served as a quarry for building materials. New partition walls, for example, made use of the salvaged tile, tubing and stone from the old structure. Close to the old *mansio* a piazza was created, around which traces of new structures were found. The timber dwellings and workshops

6. (A) Reconstruction of the later Roman *mansio* at Torrita di Siena;
(B) Reconstruction of the fifth- to sixth-century village at Torrita di
Siena in the ruins of the *mansio*.

existed into the sixth century. The presence of plentiful evidence
of craft production including metalworking suggests to the
excavators that the community engaged in a sub-regional commerce that was abruptly ended by the conflicts in the mid-sixth-
century Gothic war.

The buildings in this village are undoubtedly precursors of
those found in early medieval contexts. Using a mixture of
scavenged materials, it is evident that the knowledge of stone
construction no longer existed. Yet, like the final phase of San

Giusto, it was a settlement which could still boast involvement in regional production and distribution. Here, though, in the absence of a villa or church, we are witnessing a world of peasant craftsmen on the eve of new era.

The demise of villas and the appearance of the early medieval castle

Let us now turn to the process that led to the definitive dissolution of the villa system between the fifth and sixth centuries, the reasons for which lie mainly in the slow death of an entire cultural system. The phenomenon was not a sudden one. Although the Gothic war between Italy's Ostrogothic rulers and Byzantine imperial forces in 535-54 represented the climax of the process of villa decline, its roots lay in the inexorable provincialisation of Italy. Centre and periphery; the mountains, valleys and coastal littorals; and most of all towns and the countryside were pulling apart. The integration of the heyday of the Roman empire was well and truly over. In specific terms this involved the drain of wealth towards the provinces, the dependence of ports on foreign markets (particularly in the east Mediterranean), and the steady marginalisation of the Italic aristocracy in the imperial context. Taking a wide-angled view of these centuries, the Constantinian revival of the fourth century was reduced to little more than an episode based on the illusion that a period of political stability might solve deep-rooted problems which, to their eventual cost, the ruling classes failed to grasp (cf. Ripoll & Arce 2000).

By the sixth century, subsistence farming had become much more widespread as links between the cities and the countryside weakened. Only few areas (Ravenna, the Byzantine part of Abruzzo, Latium, Naples, Calabria and perhaps Sicily) were actively involved in Mediterranean trade (cf. Staffa 2000, for example, on the Abruzzo). The archaeology of rural settlement in this period is far from precisely known. From our snapshots, however, a picture is forming. While vestigial remains were noted in the ruins of San Giovanni di Ruoti, the *vicus* at San Vincenzo al Volturno in Molise was evidently aggregating a larger community (Hodges & Rovelli 1998). In Byzantine Liguria and in places in the Alpine foothills new fortified *castra* were being constructed – the centres of networks of fortifications for a population that was no longer rooted to the old matrix of the countryside. Further south, in Tuscany, a new settlement was being created on the hilltop at Poggibonsi, occupying an ecological niche (Valenti 1996a; 1996b).

The new archaeological evidence might imply that anarchy reigned in the countryside, where the peasants were freed from all kinds of subordination. But here we must be careful. Although on the one hand it is evident that the period analysed thus far was characterised by a progressive simplification of social structure, of production processes and of buildings, on the other, the total absence of hierarchies does not tally with the written sources or, for that matter, with the admittedly small amount of archaeological evidence. Elites most definitely had not disappeared. Recent studies of cemeteries from the sixth and seventh centuries – notably Castel Trosino and Nocera Umbra (Paroli 1997b; Rupp 1995) – where accoutrements (weapons, jewellery, glasses and pottery) associated with graves have been ranked, show a marked hierarchy, at least as far as the funerary ritual was concerned. The fact that the Lombard aristocracy appear to have been unwilling to intervene in the management of their landed properties cannot be interpreted as an absence of social hierarchy, at least until the beginning of the eighth century.

This is the moment when early medieval hilltop sites first come to our attention. In the past, *castra* such as Invillino in Friuli, and indeed, hilltop occupation in the Tiber valley, have been interpreted as a reaction to the devastating impact of the

Gothic war. As we noted at San Giovanni di Ruoti, even in Basilicata, far from the epicentre of the generation-long conflict, it has been interpreted as a watershed. Instead, we propose, the end of the old settlement system was determined not so much by the devastation wrought by the marauding armies, whose actions were generally insubstantial, but rather by the accelerated militarisation of society and the countryside. Militarisation became a critical factor of the later sixth and seventh centuries. Fortifications had always existed along the borders; following the Gothic war, though, a new feature has been identified – constantly shifting internal boundaries that determined the need to use fortified settlements in strategic locations to control the territory (Brown 1978; 1984). The examples that have received most attention from scholars are Monte Barro, Castelseprio and Monselice in Lombardy. At Monte Barro a Gothic aristocrat built the *castrum* on a series of natural terraces at 922 m above sea level; the buildings covered about 8 of the 50 hectares enclosed by the walls (Fig. 7). The principal feature of this settlement is a courtyard palace with porticoed ranges on three sides. This appears to be the seat of a major aristocrat from the mid-fifth to mid-sixth century, when the palace was destroyed in a fire (Brogiolo & Castelletti 1991). At Monte Barro, the excavators believe, a Gothic leader was living in late antique splendour with all the symbols and authority of late antiquity. The royal fortress site of Castelseprio near Milan was built at about the end of the fifth century as an important and complex centre. Its walls enclosed an area of over 6 hectares, including public buildings, dwellings and a road network. In the Lombard period, Castelseprio played a key role for a large surrounding area, becoming the administrative hub of a civil district. The fine cycle of frescoes of the church of S. Maria *foris Portas,* dating from the Carolingian period, is further testimony to the signal importance of the settlement (Gelichi 1997: 76-7; 189-91). At Monselice, the early medieval settlement

7. Reconstruction of the Gothic palace in the *castrum* of Monte Barro (Lombardy).

was established on a hill towards the end of the sixth century. The first, Byzantine, *castrum* was defended by walls enclosing an area of 3 hectares. Later, following its fall to Lombard forces, a Lombard cemetery was put here which has produced a rich collection of funerary objects dating from the first half of the seventh century.

The castles founded or re-used by the Goths, Byzantines and Lombards always originated from public power and for the purpose of defence, never from private initiative to control resources and the population, as was to happen in the later middle ages. This feature was also a limitation with respect to new settlement: once the urgent need for defence had been met, many of these places were deserted and never occupied again (cf. Staffa 2000 on the fortresses in the Abruzzo). The only centres to survive were those that managed to fulfil other functions – services that had once been delegated to the cities.

Questions arise as to how and to what degree the foundation of fortified sites affected the process of social and economic change in the countryside. What did those peasants who occupied places like Settefinestre, San Giovanni di Ruoti or San Giusto, constructing timber dwellings, make of these new central places? It is certain that the successful sites, such as Castelseprio (Varese) or Monselice (Padua), brought together the economic and administrative activities of the surrounding areas. On the other hand, the *castrum* in Monte Barro close to Milan (Brogiolo & Castelletti 1991), was deserted, as were hundreds of other small and medium-sized sites that had been fortified, invariably by re-utilising pre-Roman defences.

This is the context for a brief discussion of Lombard settlement. The arrival and subsequent migration within Italy of Lombard groups have been the subject of much debate (cf. Christie 1993). By the seventh century Lombard polities had been established in northern Italy, in the uplands around Spoleto and around the southern city of Benevento. While their cemeteries have received considerable attention, the associated settlements remain largely unknown. Moreover, at present it is not clear whether the Lombards preferred urban to rural settlement. It is furthermore difficult to make general observations as yet, because it is clear that at different phases of the invasion, the different geographical and historical contexts in which the Lombards settled, were determining factors for creating reciprocal cultural exchanges. For some scholars, the location of new Lombard settlements was connected to the imperative for defence. Their small numbers, so the argument goes, coupled with a more or less permanent state of war, were factors that conditioned settlement, limiting it to the strategic defence of roads, cities, fords and mountain passes. This hypothesis, however, has still to be proved.

Let us look at a few examples of this last chapter in the history of the landscapes of late antiquity. Throughout northern Italy, as we have already seen, villa estates began to decline during the fifth century. Some complexes, nevertheless, were partially and selectively re-planned as late as the sixth century. In the Trentino plain, for example, stone buildings were replaced by wooden constructions; at Varone the interior of a villa was used as a burial ground. Dramatic abandonment of the countryside does not seem to have taken place, although the shift of settlement towards the western hill areas might be explained by the dissolution of the old Roman system of centuriation. In Lombardy, only 12 of the 70 villas and farms known in the first century still existed in the fifth century, and, of these, 7 were occupied until the sixth century. Of course, this is little more than a small sample, illustrating the rise and fall of villas in the region. At Monzambano, after a period of decline and spoliation in the mid-fifth century, new constructions were built either in wood or pisé (clay) or a combination of the two materials. The villa at Sirmione on Lake Garda was deserted at about the end of the century; in about the same period the villa in Desenzano was destroyed by fire. At Pontevico the continuing inhabitation between the fourth and sixth centuries is characterised by buildings with stone foundations and a wooden superstructure. At the villa of Nuvoleto, following the demolition of its bath-building towards the end of the sixth century, small structures made of timber were inserted into its ruins (cf. Brogiolo 1996a).

The region of Piedmont maintained a relative prosperity at the beginning of the fifth century, as the villas of Ticeneto and Centallo demonstrate. During the century, small chapels began to appear within the villas, both in the Novara area at the villas of Carpignano and Sizzano, and in the Cuneo region at Centallo.

These chapels were often to survive well into the sixth or even the early seventh centuries. Between the end of the fifth century and the early decades of the sixth century, the Tuscan countryside also shows unequivocal signs of the selection process of the settlement network that determined the rise of new centres of population. Although the inland parts were characterised by the presence of sparse communities, coastal areas saw the transformation of maritime villas into protected maritime settlements. This is most visible in the Cosa/Ansedonia (Grosseto) area, where a combination of geographical position and the presence of ancient city walls provided natural refuge (cf. Fentress & Perkins 1989; Cambi in Carandini & Cambi 2002: 239-41). The entire border area between Tuscany and Latium was affected by the shift of episcopal sees and the formation of fortifications that stretched inland following the main roads and rivers as far as Lake Bolsena. In the middle of the sixth century it is apparent that throughout most of Tuscany there was a low density of population in a landscape characterised by open uninhabited zones alternating with areas where a closely-knit network of new isolated dwellings and structures emerged by exploiting the lands abandoned by the villas. For example, traces of a polarisation of settlements are visible along the main medieval roads, such as at Torrita di Siena (see above).

Into this new settlement pattern a network of rural churches was inserted, serving two functions. First, as nodes for the religious organisation of the countryside; secondly, as assembly points, designated by an urban aristocracy, for an increasingly scattered rural population (Brogiolo 2001). For example, at San Marcellino, in the Chianti region, the church was built on the site of a villa that was used until late antiquity. Similarly, in Latium the estate centre at the Mola di Monte Gelato was reduced to a small chapel with traces of enduring occupation in a mausoleum close by (Fig. 8). By contrast, in Molise a small

57

hilltop chapel at Colle Sant'Angelo, overlooking San Vincenzo al Volturno, attests the increasing christianisation of the mostly abandoned Roman landscapes (Hodges 1997).

In Latium the late antique settlement network proved to be stronger than elsewhere. There are, however, interesting discrepancies between what has emerged from the South Etruria survey on the one hand, and what has been observed from the number of churches (approximately 30) and cemeteries of late antiquity and the early middle ages (26) in the region. The South Etruria survey points to a severe phase of depopulation, which is to some extent contradicted by the number of churches and cemeteries (cf. Potter 1979). On the other hand, the known cemeteries cover large areas, implying that they were used by a number of settlements. For example, between the sixth and seventh centuries, the necropolis of Rignano Flaminio contained about 500-600 graves and has yet to be associated within any settlement. Concurrently there was a collapse of the regional marketing system, as John Hayes has noted: 'the total ARS [African Red Slip] finds from the period *c.* 470-550 are a third of what they had been in the early to mid-fifth century, and about a tenth of the fourth-century figure. After 550 these imports disappear almost completely, and local substitutes, if any, are rare' (Hayes 1998: 13).

To the east, in the Teramano area of the region of Abruzzo, both the Gothic war and the Lombard invasion considerably influenced forms of settlement. Buildings constructed in late antiquity were re-used as dwellings or cemeteries. In the lower Pescara valley the occupation of ancient sites has been linked to a continuing Byzantine presence up until the early decades of the seventh century (Staffa 2000). During this period considerable agricultural restructuring took place in order to supply the neighbouring Byzantine coastal towns of *Castrum Truentinum*, *Castrum Novum*, *Ostia*, *Aternum*, *Hortona* and *Histonium*. Ports seem to have remained in use until the mid-

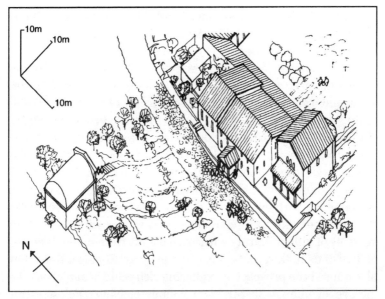

8. Reconstruction of Mola di Monte Gelato (Latium) in the sixth century.

seventh century, thanks in large part to their role in supplying Byzantine garrisons with goods from the eastern Mediterranean (cf. Volpe 1998).

In Apulia, too, there exists strong evidence of settlement discontinuity determined by the war between the Goths and the Byzantines, and exacerbated by the later Lombard invasion. Settlement discontinuity was the consequence both of the conquest and of the conflict itself. Here, the mid-sixth century was a period of severe crisis in the countryside: in the Salento area and the Oria district desertion was widespread; on the Gargano peninsula numerous settlements were re-occupied by small, often poor, communities judging by the remains of buildings in recycled wood or stone. In some cases (Avicenna, Melfi-Leonessa, Campi Salentina-Santa Maria dell'Alto, S. Miserino and Rutigliano-Purgatorio), during the sixth and seventh centuries, new villages developed around small religious buildings built on or near older villas. The case of S. Giusto is an excellent example, as we saw above.

Three different zones therefore co-existed on the Italian peninsula, each with a different economic organisation. First, an inland area with relatively simple forms of settlement, typically *vici*, which we might interpret as villages, where subsistence farming was carried out. Secondly, inland areas where settlement was linked to production for the centres under Byzantine imperial authority. Thirdly, the coastal littorals and their immediate hinterlands, where a number of large settlements, with evidence of élite residences, still survived. As the world of late antiquity ebbed away, and with it the last vestiges of villa life, Italy witnessed a shift from mixed farming on lowlands to the occupation of defensively sited locations that also offered the prospect of exploiting rich ecological niches. The picture of change is far from complete. Nevertheless, after twenty years of intensive research, there is a sense that the end of antiquity brought about not only new cultural mores but also a return to places that had been settled before the Graeco-Roman world imposed its order on the peninsula.

The Beginnings of Hilltop Villages

... despite their institutionalisation in the practice of archaeology and history, the silenced Voice, the mute Artifact, and the all-knowing Word are *recent* phenomena. ... we sacrifice any hope of really understanding the past if we impose on it conceptions of the Object, Voice and Word which are of such recent historicity. I would contend that we simply cannot understand any historical past if we 'exalt the primacy of the word to the level of the eternal' and simply assume that the object-world is mute. For most of the historic past we have little hope of directly recovering the words of the Voice, but the techniques and theory of modern archaeology enable us to understand the meanings of Objects. (Moreland 2001a: 75-6)

Introduction

Few archaeologists and historians any longer doubt the picture of villa decline described in the previous chapter. Mute artifacts convey the overwhelming sense of rural transformation. There is no real debate other than about the social and economic circumstances that caused this to happen. The debate focusses on what happened next. Put simply: was there some kind of dispersed settlement pattern until the advent of *incastellamento* in the tenth century, or did the *castelli* described in

tenth-century foundation charters owe their origins to an undocumented moment when, with the demise of the Roman
landscape, the medieval one took shape? As we explained in
Chapter 1, we contend that in many cases the hilltop village –
best known from picture-postcard places in Tuscany and
Umbria – owes its origin to the sixth to seventh centuries. In
this chapter we aim to review the evidence to support this
hypothesis.

The search for Dark Age type fossils

The key to this debate is of course the ability to date archaeological sites. Once John Hayes provided a chronology for African Red Slip ware (1972), for example, it became a great deal
easier not only to recognise later Roman sites and levels in
excavations, but also to date them. In many ways Hayes' research revolutionised the study of late antiquity (cf. Ward-
Perkins 2001). But around the seventh century the distinctive
imported tablewares and amphorae became increasingly scarce
outside major maritime centres in Italy. Indeed, as Hayes himself noted, African Red Slip wares appear to disappear even in
the hinterland of Rome after *c*. 550 (1998). Until the excavations
of the Crypta Balbi in Rome during the 1990s produced a
largely uninterrupted coin-dated sequence of ceramics stretch-
ing from the seventh to the tenth century, it was extremely
difficult to date the pottery of this period (cf. Manacorda 2001:
44-52). Considerable effort was invested in dating funerary pots
found in Lombard cemeteries, and using these as indices for
dating settlement sites. To complicate matters still further,
accoutrements were rarely placed in Lombard graves after the
third quarter of the seventh century, so dating funerary pots by
association with jewellery had its limitations. The search for
type fossils was led, as Chris Wickham has recently noted, by
David Whitehouse who began by studying the assemblage of

wares from the ninth-century *domusculta* of Santa Cornelia, near Rome, found in the South Etruria survey (Wickham 2001). Whitehouse set up a floating typology of early medieval broad-line and narrow-line red-painted wares, and at the same time placed great emphasis upon ninth-century Forum ware (Fig. 9), a distinctive lead-glazed ceramic found in and around Rome (cf. Gelichi 1997: 65). Whitehouse's pioneering studies paved the way for a succession of other floating typologies of early medieval wares. In the Abruzzo, Lombardy, Tuscany and Molise similar typologies of ceramic forms have now been proposed. Initially these were based on stratigraphic sequences, or, in the case of Molise, on the historically-dated deposits found at the Benedictine monastery of San Vincenzo al Volturno (Patterson 2001).

Using these ceramic typologies, as yet only a handful of sites help us to chart the next stage in the history of rural settlement. All of them lead us to propose that the inhabitants of the small nucleated villages of later antiquity invariably but not always abandoned the 'classical landscape' and moved to occupy defensive locations on hilltops.

Casale San Donato

In an attempt to test alternative visions of the early medieval Italian countryside, John Moreland developed a programme of field survey and excavation in the region between the Benedictine monastery of Farfa in the Sabine Hills, east of Rome, and the Tiber valley (Moreland & Pluciennik 1991; Moreland *et al.* 1993; Moreland 2001b). The Farfa survey, as it was known, showed that this region was densely populated at the zenith of the Roman empire, much like South Etruria. However, the initial failure to locate sites of the sixth to eighth century could be seen as confirmation of theories of dramatic depopulation and collapse. With the disappearance of diagnostic Roman fine

9. Two examples of ninth-century Forum ware from the Forum of Rome.

wares such as African Red Slip, new chronological markers had to be discovered to determine the fate of the communities in this area. Excavations at Casale San Donato, near Castelnuovo di Farfa, not only provided such a 'marker'; they also provided an unusual insight into the organisation of settlement and society.

Texts in the Farfa monastic archive give an immediate impression of the significance of San Donato. In 768 a widow called Taneldis donated the *fundus Cicilianus* to the monastery of Farfa, while a document of 817 records the *fundum Cicilianum in quo est aecclesia sancti Donati*. By the mid-eighth century, Farfa had acquired the area within which the site of San Donato is situated. In fact, it is possible that by this time the embryonic monastery already held significant possessions in this part of the Sabine Hills. Two texts of 746 record that Lupus, Duke of Spoleto, ceded to Farfa first a portion and then the whole of the *gualdus* of San Giacinto. These texts make a connection between this *gualdus* and the place called *Agellum*, while the 817 document referred to above makes an explicit link between San Donato and *Agellum – Fundum Agellum Fundum Cicilianum in quo est aecclesia sancti donati* (Moreland 2001b).

The archaeological evidence from the site confirms its significance. Excavations at San Donato revealed two major phases of construction and habitation, the earliest of which predates the first record of the site in the monastic archive. This early phase consisted of several post-built structures situated on the side of the small hill. Buildings may also have covered the top of the hill, but these have been destroyed by later activity. Also associated with this phase were a series of intercutting pits which contained notable amounts of ceramics and animal bones, as well as fragments of soapstone, glass vessels and bone combs. Indeed, at least fourteen types of pottery, mostly produced locally, but some known from coin-dated deposits found in the excavations of the Crypta Balbi, Rome, illustrate the scale and

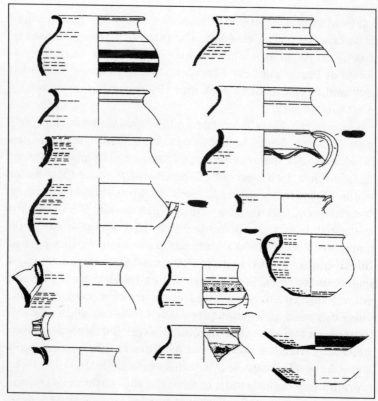

10. A selection of late sixth/seventh-century ceramics from Casale San Donato.

extent of production, distribution and consumption (Fig. 10). Apart from some re-used architectural pieces, Roman material culture is entirely absent from the site and it seems that it was a new foundation of the late sixth and seventh centuries.

Cutting through, and therefore post-dating, this phase was a large stone wall, which turned a right angle within the area of the excavation. To the south of this wall were found the remains of two kilns, the size of which would suggest that they were used for the manufacture of tiles or bricks. Moreland has proposed (and this can only be confirmed by more detailed analysis of the stratigraphic sequence) that this phase might be associated with Farfa's acquisition of the site in 768, and that the wall formed a terrace on which it constructed a series of buildings – including the church referred to in 817. The aggrandisement of the site evident in the switch from building in wood to stone construction may be a physical manifestation of the power of the monastery in the area surrounding its new acquisition.

The ceramics are the key to our appreciation of the significance of San Donato. These provide the date for the foundation of the site, and permit us to re-enter the debate on the fate of the central Italian countryside in the transition from late antiquity to the middle ages. The existence of San Donato in the late sixth/seventh century confirms the impression we gain from the (ninth-century) documents that the countryside was not abandoned and depopulated. Moreover, further analysis of the field survey material in the light of the San Donato ceramics provides us with a more nuanced picture of changes in the pattern of settlement in the Sabine Hills. While few sites show real continuity from the late Roman period onwards, San Donato is one of 11 new foundations of the late sixth/seventh century. This reorientation of settlement occurred in the context of the emergence of new regional patterns of production and distribution, of which the San Donato ceramics are themselves the prime exemplar. It is perhaps significant that both developments are contemporary with the arrival of the Lombards in the region.

The second phase of occupation at San Donato may be connected with its acquisition and expansion by Farfa. If the same can be demonstrated on other sites acquired by the monastery at this time, it might suggest an investment in, and reorganisation, of its productive hinterland in either the second half of the eighth or the early ninth century, similar to developments happening elsewhere in Italy (as we shall illustrate in Chapter 4). Finally, we should note that San Donato was later involved in the *incastellamento* process – a text of 1046 refers to it as a *castellum* (cf. Hubert 2000: 11).

Montarrenti, Poggibonsi and Scarlino

Three Tuscan villages excavated on a large scale over the past twenty years provide exemplars of the shift from dispersed lowland settlement to hilltops.

Montarrenti is situated on a low hill about 20 km. west of Siena. It controls a fertile valley that had sustained modest farms during the Roman period. Excavations of a significant sample of the hilltop and the ring of terraced midslope dwellings showed that it was occupied from the mid-seventh century until the present day, with several fine Romanesque tower-houses attesting to its heyday in the twelfth to fifteenth centuries. The excavations show that, in the mid-seventh to mid- to late eighth-century village, there were small rectangular huts situated on the hilltop within a defensive palisade, and probably huts of similar date on a lower terrace outside the fortification (Fig. 11). The size of the village is difficult to estimate from the sample. Suffice it to note that post-built structures were discovered in each of the three excavation areas on the midslope, suggesting that the village numbered many buildings. The material culture was poor, quite unlike that of Casale San Donato. Simple cooking pots, jugs and hand-made *testi* – large plates – comprised the greater part of an assemblage which was evidently made locally (Cantini 2003).

The site of Poggio Imperiale, the hilltop overlooking modern Poggibonsi in central Tuscany, is a settlement which at its zenith in the ninth century covered at least two hectares. The excavator ascribes its beginnings to the sixth to seventh centuries. From this evolved a village that perhaps owes its early history to the involvement of the monastery of Marturi. A notable feature of the village is its unplanned character, lending

3. The Beginnings of Hilltop Villages

11. Hypothetical reconstruction of Montarrenti (Tuscany) in the eighth to ninth centuries.

weight to the proposal that it grew up spontaneously until the ninth century. The earliest structures are rectangular and post-built; they were frequently rebuilt. No traces of defences have been found. Its material culture, in common with Montarrenti, was simple and locally produced (Valenti 1996a; 1996b).

Scarlino occupies a prominent hilltop in western Tuscany overlooking the sea. The village boasts a major thirteenth-century castle belonging to the commune of Pisa, below which excavations were made in the late 1970s and early 1980s. Much of the hill of Scarlino, unlike Montarrenti and Poggibonsi, is still inhabited today. The hilltop was first occupied in the later Bronze Age as well as during the Etruscan and Hellenistic periods. In Roman times the port of Scabris was located below on the coastline, and led to the desertion of the hill. In AD 973 it was a *castello* of the Aldobrandeschi counts. Before this, however, two phases of occupation were identified. The earliest, dating to the seventh to eighth centuries, consists of post-built structures similar to those at Montarrenti and Poggibonsi, which were superseded by an arrangement of structures with an associated small church that appears to be a ninth-century estate centre (*curtis*) (cf. Cantini 2003; Francovich 1985; Valenti 1996a).

San Vincenzo al Volturno and Vacchereccia

The later Roman estate centre at San Vincenzo al Volturno appears to have prospered well into the sixth century (Hodges & Rovelli 1998) and overall, like many classical settlements in the eastern Abruzzo identified by Andrea Staffa (2000), was continuously occupied from the early Samnite period in the sixth century BC up to the twelfth century AD. A fifth- to sixth-century tower within the estate centre, however, was deserted by the middle to later part of the sixth century. Its funerary church, too, no longer functioned after this date. Possibly like San Giovanni di Ruoti (Basilicata) and many villages in central Italy, it was a victim of the unrest caused by the Gothic war (see Chapter 2). Nevertheless, graves cut into the tower show that it was still a reference point for a community as late as the seventh century. This may explain why it was selected by the three Benedictine founders of the monastery of San Vincenzo al Volturno in AD 703. The twelfth-century *Chronicon Vulturnense* provides a vivid description of the political ups and downs within this enclosed community. The first nucleus of simple mud and stone structures was aggregated around the earlier funerary church, possibly creating a simple rectangular complex covering little more than half a hectare (cf. Hodges 1997). Built into the side of the hill, and with the river Volturno on its east flank, it occupied, in effect, a modest defensive location.

3. The Beginnings of Hilltop Villages

The monastery provides a modest illustration of the impoverished building traditions in this part of the Duchy of Benevento, utterly different, for example, to the grand and elegant ducal buildings associated with the Lombard Duchy of Spoleto (cf. Emerick 1998). Nevertheless, the use of stone walls bonded with clay (as opposed to lime mortar), simple plastered walls and crudely mortared floors, evidently distinguished the monastery as a central place from the post-built dwellings of villages like Casale San Donato, Montarrenti, Poggibonsi and Scarlino. The only possible village of this date found in the survey of the upper Volturno valley lies at Vacchereccia, 4 km to the south-west. A tenth-century charter issued by the monastery attests that this was a modest example of *incastellamento*, but midslope traces of a post-built structure on a terrace by a defunct spring found in the 1982 excavations hint – perhaps no more – that the hill was occupied from the sixth or seventh centuries by households who had deserted the Rocchetta plain below (Hodges 1997).

A pattern?

Is there a pattern here? Are these settlements the exception or the rule? If so, they not only undermine Pierre Toubert's contention (based on the Word, to paraphrase Moreland (2001a)) that *incastellamento* was focussed on sites created *de novo* in the tenth century, but taken together with the new evidence from the field survey and the suggested developments in the eighth or early ninth centuries (based on the Object), it also spans the rupture he envisaged between late antiquity and the middle ages. If fact, they are the generalised arguments for both continuity and catastrophe must fall in the face of the new and sophisticated understandings of regional patterns of settlement and economy.

A general survey of the Adriatic littoral of the Abruzzo by

71

Andrea Staffa appears to confirm that a number of Byzantine sites, like San Vincenzo al Volturno, continued to be occupied throughout the seventh to tenth centuries (2000). Equally Staffa shows that hilltop towns such as Lanciano owe their origins to the end of Byzantine rule when undistinguished post-built structures were first erected. In a region that suffered from a near continual state of war, some villages managed to take root and prosper; others were destined to fail. Nearer to Rome, the evidence, such as it is from hilltop sites such as Ponte Nepesino excavated by Potter and Whitehouse, tends to affirm the sequence found at Casale San Donato. Further north, in the Valdinievole in north-west Tuscany, Quirós Castillo has found numerous historical references to sites such as the *vico Civilano* in 746, the *vico Colona* in 760, and the *vico Villa* in 797 (1999: 37; 51-73). Substantial excavations, however, at Terrazzana, a hilltop site in the area, revealed a small village of simple post-built structures reminiscent of Montarrenti.

At the royal centres of Castelseprio and Monselice there was undoubtedly a continuation of occupation from late antiquity, though on what scale we cannot yet say. Similarly on the fertile slopes areas around Lake Garda, near Verona, field survey shows that villages grew up in places inhabited since late antiquity. In particular, the presence of sixth- to seventh-century Lombard cemeteries close to villages first described in the age of *incastellamento* leads us to suppose, on the basis of places such as Casale San Donato, Montarrenti, Poggibonsi and Scarlino, that their origins lay in the end of late antiquity. In Piedmont, too, archaeological research has begun to uncover the first evidence of a similar pattern.

Conclusion

Notwithstanding the difficulties of dating the sites of this period, it now seems fairly clear that a dramatic shift in the settlement pattern took place in the later sixth or early seventh centuries. All the evidence points to a new centralised form of settlement being created, invariably on defensive hilltop locations, replacing the earlier dispersed pattern of inhabitation. The precise date of the settlement shift, not unlike the so-called Middle Saxon shuffle of rural settlement in southern England (Hodges 1989: 58-64) or the creation of new nucleated settlement in the earlier Merovingian period (Steuer 1989), has yet to be fixed throughout Italy. However, as we have seen, some telling examples of this critical phase in the history of Italy are now coming to light. The picture that is emerging also resembles a growing body of evidence from the Balkans where hilltop villages begin to supersede dispersed classical-period sites in precisely this period (Bowden & Hodges forthcoming). In common with Albania and Anglo-Saxon England, to take two very different European regions, the circumstances in Italy need to be more closely pinpointed. Plainly the existence of villages without the presence of lords begs a number of historical questions. So, where were the élite at this time? Were the Lombards only in the largely defunct towns, or were they managing estate centres which in some shape or other resembled either Castelseprio or San Vincenzo al Volturno?

The evidence amassed to date is difficult to assess because the buildings are undistinguished in their architectural form. Most are simple post-built structures, irregular in their oval or rectangular shape. While internal divisions were found at Montarrenti and Poggibonsi, for example, it is too early to conclude much from such observations. However, these are not examples of the fine carpentry evident in structures of the Merovingian, Anglo-Saxon or Danish late Iron Ages. And just as the buildings lack any artisanal finesse, so we must note the poverty of the material culture. As excavations of the seventh- to eighth-century rubbish middens in the Crypta Balbi, Rome, show, and the striking results from Casale San Donato confirm, this was not in fact an impoverished age in terms of material culture. A variety of ceramic tableware and storage forms existed, as did Alpine soapstone jars, fine jewellery and bonework, but plainly the distribution systems had collapsed in the sixth century. Instead, there is a sense of groups of peasants occupying woodland niches and taking advantage, as Vito Fumagalli suggested, of the rich potential for a domestic mode of production in such contexts (1987: 21-35). But it would be a mistake in the light of the new evidence to infer from the Object and silence of the Word that the peasantry had been reduced to aboriginal conditions. Quite the contrary. It is tempting to see the shift to hilltops as an initiative that took into account the distant memory of pre-Roman settlement in these places. This was an adaptive strategy, after all, that proved to be an enduring success as first the creation of the *curtis* and then the *castelli* were soon to demonstrate.

From *Curtis* to *Castello*

> The world that Charlemagne knew firsthand was peopled
> not only by Franks, Alamannians, and Saxons, by Danes,
> Anglo-Saxons, Lombards, and Visigoths, but by Venetians,
> Arabs, Jews, Byzantines, and Slavs. Perhaps never again
> in its history would Europe be so culturally open, in so
> many directions, in so many ways. (McCormick 2001: 797)

When Charlemagne led his forces south to Rome, having conquered Lombardy, he encountered a landscape that must have
puzzled him. On the one hand there were the ruins of the
Roman age, which up to the nineteenth century caused travellers to marvel. On the other hand, much of the landscape was
uncultivated and wooded. Occupying islands in this sylvan sea
were estate centres and small, nucleated villages with utterly
undistinguished architecture. Passing close to the monastery of
Farfa in the Sabine Hills, he might even have spied Casale San
Donato with its ensemble of timber and stone buildings (see
Chapter 3). He cannot have been impressed, knowing – as we
know now – the scale of Frankish manors and their villages. In
some ways, we might imagine him saying, Italy had been caught
in a time warp. Change was needed! Whether, of course, Charlemagne provided the impetus to revitalise the Italian countryside, or whether, as is more commonly believed, the Lombards
through peer-polity pressure generated a revival in their landscape, is an issue outside the scope of this book. Suffice it to note,

nonetheless, that in the later eighth century great and lasting changes occurred in Italian rural settlement.

In this chapter we shall examine the evidence for the creation of the *curtis* in the light of excavations over the past twenty years, and then, finally, how, the *castelli* of the seigneurial lordship took shape in the tenth and eleventh centuries, completing the transformation from the villa to the village.

The creation of the *curtis*

Pierre Toubert, in his classic study of Italian villages, identified *incastellamento* as a rupture with the past. Preceding *incastellamento*, according to Toubert, was a phase characterised by *curtes*, in essence manors that in his opinion were largely isolated, dispersed settlements. Prior to the Frankish invasion in the later eighth century, Toubert describes an aboriginal world in which the peasantry occupied dispersed households, *casale*. The origins of these households, although Toubert himself does not specify this, are commonly attributed to the demise of the classical settlement system in the sixth or seventh century. Toubert's model, as was noted in Chapter 1, is fundamentally about the rise of local power and their changing relations with the peasantry.

As we have seen, the archaeological evidence challenges Toubert's notion of a peasantry that lived in scattered, isolated farmsteads. Instead, in many parts of Italy – as indeed in the Frankish territories and many regions of Byzantium – nucleated and dependent dispersed farmsteads of late antiquity moved to occupy new locations in the sixth or seventh centuries. The new settlements consisted of clusters of individual farms separated by fences. It seems beyond doubt that the estate system of the *villa rustica* – predominant in Roman times – was in the early middle ages replaced by a new basic unit of production, that is by peasant households cooperating as villages. So, given this new model, where was the *curtis* situated?

We begin with the villages described in Chapter 3. What happened to them in the later eighth and ninth centuries?

At Casale San Donato in the Sabine Hills, Moreland identified a switch from timber to stone structures in the eighth century. The dating of the switch is not precise, so he associated the new buildings with the acquisition of the site by the abbey of Farfa in 768. He notes, however, that the first church is mentioned in a charter of 817. The evidence is not really sufficient to shed light on the beginnings of a *curtis* here. We must note, nonetheless, that in other Italian rural sites, as we shall see below, the switch from timber to stone structures belongs to an important change in their economic and social circumstances.

At Montarrenti, the hilltop village close in the Val d'Elsa west of Siena, a new stone enclosure wall replaced the earlier timber palisade around the hilltop during the later eighth century (Fig. 12). In the excavation area on the summit – Area 1000 – the post-built dwelling of the first phase was dismantled and a large granary was erected in its stead. Next to it was constructed a grain-drying oven. The granary was eventually destroyed in a conflagration during the ninth century. On the midslope, in Area 2000, it is not clear whether the early palisade enclosure was also replaced by a stone version. However, the post-built dwelling of the earliest phase was re-made with simple stone bonded with clay – an architectural transformation recalling the switch in building forms found at Casale San Donato. These alterations strongly suggest that the seigneurial presence, so conspicuous at Montarrenti from the later periods in the form of the elegant tower-houses on the summit, owed its origins to the later eighth or ninth century when a new fortification and, significantly, a building dedicated to the storage of grain was established here.

77

12. Hypothetical reconstruction of Montarrenti (Tuscany) in the ninth to tenth centuries.

At Poggibonsi the alterations made in this period are more striking. A new planned village was imposed upon the earlier settlement, with a longhouse and associated structures being at the heart of the new community (Fig. 13). A road made of beaten earth led from this new complex through the settlement, either side of which were timber structures with post-built and earth-fast timber walls. The longhouse is, of course, a notable discovery. The bow-shaped building was 19 m long and 8 m wide. Within its fenced enclosure were found the remains of a barn similar in some respects to the barn found at Montarrenti, as well as a slaughterhouse. The ceramics, like those from Montarrenti, reveal local production and in many respects are unexceptional. However, an important faunal assemblage was

13. Reconstruction of the ninth-century longhouse at Poggibonsi (Tuscany).

associated with this building. From it we may deduce that the household was consuming only better cuts of meat, particularly beef. In other words, they benefited from a selective production process that had occurred elsewhere within the settlement. The assemblage is quite different to that found in the surrounding dwellings where poorer quality parts of animals, such as their feet, for example, were being consumed. Indeed, in dwelling 1 cattle bones were absent altogether (Valenti 1996a; 1996b).

At Scarlino overlooking the Maremma coast, again dating to the later eighth or early ninth centuries, it is clear that a new concentration of buildings was created on the summit of the hill

14. Hypothetical reconstruction of the *curtis* at Scarlino (Tuscany).

(Fig. 14). The remains are not as deeply stratified as at Montarrenti or Poggibonsi. Nonetheless, it is evident that a new nucleus of timber structures, probably with an accompanying axially-aligned church made of rubble bonded with clay – its apse decorated with frescoes – represented a new authority in the settlement. The presence of lead glazed wares (so-called sparse glazed pottery) in the uppermost levels associated with the desertion of these buildings points to an abandonment no later than AD 973, when it is described as a *curtis*. Like Montarrenti and Poggibonsi, the material culture is notable for the absence of long-distance imports of any kind. In contrast to Casale San Donato, soapstone and extra-regional types of pottery were absent (Francovich 1985).

Two other sites merit our attention before we examine other classes of rural settlement from this period.

4. From Curtis to Castello

The first of these is Santa Maria in Civita, a hilltop site in the Biferno valley overlooking a bridging point, 30 km from the Adriatic sea. Santa Maria in Civita, when it was first identified, was interpreted as a classic ninth-century hilltop village in which timber and simple stone dwellings were found built up against an enclosure wall (Fig. 15) (Hodges, Barker & Wade 1980; Hodges & Wickham 1995). A subsequent re-evaluation shows that the site comprises two enclosures with an associated church, situated on the highest point on the hill (Bowes & Hodges 2002). Traces of a modest tower now appear to exist in the eastern enclosure, where excavations in 1978 brought to light grain storage pits (see Hodges & Wickham 1995). Detailed analysis of the grain and its weeds showed that it was the product of processing that had taken place elsewhere. These excavations also brought to light a modestly affluent material culture that included glass vessels. Note should also be taken of the presence of bricks and tiles which were very probably made here for specific building projects. Viewed through the prism of the Latium and Tuscan sites described above, Santa Maria in

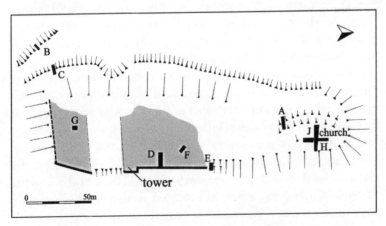

15. Plan of the settlement at Santa Maria in Civita (Molise) showing the 1978 excavation trenches, the church and the two habitation areas (shaded).

81

Civita was certainly not a hilltop village. Instead, it appears to have been a ninth-century Beneventan élite settlement comprising a household unit (the eastern enclosure) concentrated around a modest tower, an ancillary unit (the western enclosure) and its own church. Santa Maria in Civita was not a *castrum* in the sense of defending a bridge-head (of the type known from the sixth century during the Gothic war (cf. Brown 1978; 1984)), for its tower overlooked its southern side rather than the nearby Ponte San Antuono; nor was it in form a classical farm. This said, it appears to have been the centre of an estate associated with either farms or villages in the vicinity. In appearance this might appear to be the kind of dispersed manorial unit that Pierre Toubert had in mind as a *curtis* (cf. 1983). Thanks to the distinctive ceramics found in the excavations of Santa Maria in Civita, we may be confident that the later Roman farms found in the Biferno valley survey in this area did not continue until the ninth century. No dispersed sites with ninth-century potsherds were found in the survey; evidently, as was noted in Chapter 2, dispersed lowland occupation ceased by the seventh century at latest (Hodges & Wickham 1995). In short, as with the longhouse at Poggibonsi, we are witnessing a new settlement type, being introduced into a post-classical mode of farming the landscape.

Santa Maria in Civita was almost certainly destroyed in a conflagration, perhaps by the Arabs who raided in the Biferno valley in the 880s. Possibly some of its functions were assumed by Guardialfiera, a hilltop village situated 3 km to the north.

An analogous settlement was found in the neighbouring Volturno valley during the project designed to examine the terra of the Benedictine monastery of San Vincenzo al Volturno. At Colle Castellano, a low hill located in the southern, fertile zone of the terra, excavations revealed the presence of a small stone-built tower close to the summit of the hill associated with later ninth- or early tenth-century ceramics (pottery dated by association with the levels found at San Vincenzo belonging to the Arab sack of 10 October 881 (Hodges 1997)). The tower measured approximately 5 x 5 m. The excavations were too limited to determine whether timber structures were associated. However, the tower was obliterated when a new, well-made enclosure wall was constructed around the hilltop, almost certainly in the period after AD 945 when the hill, known as Olivella, was designated as a *castellum*. As in the Tuscan villages described above, the process of *incastellamento* here evidently involved a reorganisation of the settlement.

Clearly, the territories of the abbeys of Farfa (in which Casale San Donato lay), of Marturi (in which Poggibonsi was situated), and of San Vincenzo al Volturno (in which Colle Castellano was located) were not exceptional in fostering the phenomenon of the *curtis*. In Tuscany, the abbey of San Salvatore on Monte Amiata, founded in the eighth century, had by the ninth century expanded its territorial influence westwards as far as the Tyrrhenian coast by means of *cellae*, small dependent monasteries, that functioned on the model of the *curtis*. In Lombardy the monastery of Santa Giulia at Brescia was also developing the *curtis* system. Elsewhere in the Italian peninsula it is clear that significant changes were occurring in the structure of villages. Around Lake Garda Gian-Pietro Brogiolo has noted a change in village topography from this moment, just as it has been found to the west in Piedmont (Brogiolo 1996b). In the upland, chestnut woods north of Lucca, Quirós Castillo (1999) has identified changes to villages such as Terrazzana; in the Abruzzo, the sweeping survey of early medieval settlement history by Andrea Staffa (2000) shows a similar pattern with, for example, grain storage pits like those from Santa Maria in Civita occurring in the hilltop town of Lanciano (Staffa 1994: fig. 72). In Latium, in the hinterland of Rome, the powerful presence of what Peter Llewellyn called the pope-presidents is all too evident, as we shall illustrate below (Llewellyn 1986). Further south, within the sphere of first Byzantine and then Arab hegemony, in Apulia and Sicily, the situation in the countryside was rather different. In inland Apulia it appears that rural settlement was generally abandoned between the seventh and tenth centuries, probably in favour of the ports on the Adriatic coast (for example, Bari, Barletta, Otranto and Trani). Judging from Giuliano Volpe's survey of northern Apulia, widespread re-occupation and a vast re-population of the countryside took place only from the eleventh century onwards following a Byzantine imperial initiative (Martin 1980; Volpe 1998). In Sicily, field surveys in the western parts of the island around Monreale, Entella and Eraclea Minoa, show an increase in the desertion of sites around the fifth century, with a survival of the larger settlements on which, notably, fourth- to seventh-century African Red Slip wares and ninth- to tenth-century polychrome glazed wares have been come to light. The population, it seems, was grouped in villages based on the late antique settlement network. Survey close to the classical city of Segesta confirms this picture. Interestingly, the Arab invasion of the ninth century appears not to have caused any rupture. However, many lowland nucleated centres began to decline between the end of the tenth and the beginning of the eleventh century when it became necessary to build fortifications (Molinari 1994).

The *domuscultae* and San Vincenzo al Volturno

Three sites discovered in recent years, however, beg the question of dispersed, non-hilltop settlement and continuity beyond the end of late antiquity. These are the two ninth-century *domuscultae* of Latium, and the late Roman estate centre and early medieval monastery at San Vincenzo al Volturno (Molise). In this section let us examine these places in the light of our general thesis about the transition from the villa to the village.

As we noted in Chapter 1, the discovery and excavations of

the ninth-century papal farm (the *domusculta* Capracorum) at Santa Cornelia, north of Rome, proved to be a crucial part in the development of medieval archaeology in Italy. Santa Cornelia appeared to be a solitary complex, its architecture seemingly modelled upon town-housing in nearby Rome, and its prototype perhaps being a *villa rustica* of classical times. Closer inspection suggests that, in fact, it is a kind of manorial complex, not dissimilar to Santa Maria in Civita or the longhouse complex at Poggibonsi (Fig. 16).

The *Liber Pontificalis* records that Pope Hadrian I (772-95) founded six *domuscultae* in the environs of Rome. In doing this Hadrian was imitating the policy of Pope Zacharias (741-52), who had created four such estates, extending from a location 20 km north of Rome to Anzio, and possibly Gaeta, in the south. The purpose of these *domuscultae* has been much debated. Ostensibly they were intended to help feed the poor of Rome. More recently, however, Zacharias' foundations have been interpreted as an attempt to counter the economic losses caused by the confiscation of all the papacy's holdings in southern Italy and Sicily by the Byzantine emperor, Leo III, in *c.* 730 and possibly by the increasing aggression of the Lombards who had secured lands in the territory of Sutri (in 728-9) and in the Tiber valley close to Amelia, Orte, Bomarzo and Bieda in 738-9.

These were not necessarily agricultural foundations in unoccupied land. Wickham contended that Capracorum was composed of existing farms, both inherited and purchased (1979). Only the church was a new addition to the property. Indeed, the acquisition of the new estates was a source of conflict. In 815 several newly-founded *domuscultae* were sacked by Romans whose land 'had been taken from them contrary to the law'.

The actual extent of the lands of the *domuscultae* has been much debated. Wickham believes that the farms comprised unconnected fragments of farms and lands. None of these papal

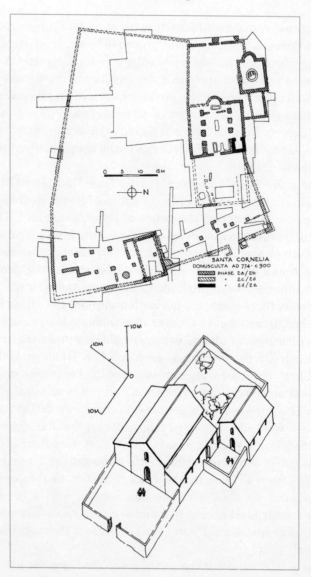

16. Sketch plan of the *domusculta* at Santa Cornelia and reconstruction of the eighth-century church.

estates, however, would have been comparable to the great villa estates of the early Roman imperial period. This said, little is known about the physical relationship of these places to the core of the estate. Accordingly we do not fully understand the mechanics of their organisation. Was the produce of each place transported directly to Rome, or was it first accumulated in storehouses? The *Liber Pontificalis* appears to record that produce was regularly despatched to warehouses in Rome. Was the network of estates managed as a coordinated enterprise? Certainly in the turbulent aftermath of the Arab sack of Rome in 846 during which St Peter's was burnt, Pope Leo IV summoned the peasantry from the *domuscultae* to build a circuit around the Vatican, known as the Leonine Wall. A surviving inscription attests to the militia or crews from the estate of Capracorum which, under the supervisor (corrector) Agatho, constructed a tower and a stretch of wall. Another inscription describes the building of two towers and a length of wall by the militia from the otherwise unknown *domuscultae* of Saltasina.

This was not the only deployment of the network of *domuscultae* as a force. In 824 Pope Paschal I used part of the workforce to counter a potential uprising by his chief clerk (*primicerius*), Theodore, and his son-in-law Leo.

Capracorum – Santa Cornelia

The *Liber Pontificalis* describes the *domusculta* of Capracorum, founded about 776 by Pope Hadrian I, as follows:

> The same most holy Pope [Hadrian I] created and founded four papal estates, of which one is called Capracorum, in the territory of Veii, about 15 miles out of Rome. Of this estate, the original farm of Capracorum together with several other farms adjoining it, was his own property, inherited from his family; and to it he added a number of

other estates, giving just compensation for each to the persons from whom he bought them. This *domusculta* of Capracorum, with its *massae* [lands], *fundi* [farms], *casales* [farm buildings], vineyards, olive groves, water-mills and all else appertaining to it, be established under apostolic privilege and with the sanction of solemn penalties, that it should for all time continue to be applied to the use of our brothers in Christ, the poor; and that the wheat and barley grown each year in its fields should be carefully collected and stored apart in the granary of our holy church. The wine, too, and the vegetables grown each year in the domains and fields of the aforesaid *domusculta*, should similarly be diligently collected and stored separately in the storehouse of our holy church. And of the pigs which should each year be fattened in the *casales* in the said *domusculta*, one hundred head should be slaughtered and stored in the same storehouse. (Duchesne 1886, I, 501-2)

Capracorum was identified in the spring of 1960 during the course of the South Etruria survey (cf. Potter 1979). The 1960-4 excavations revealed no evidence of a Roman villa beneath the early medieval estate centre. However, traces of trenches of Roman date, possibly for olives or vines, criss-crossed the site, indicating the presence of a Roman farm hereabouts. To build the *domusculta* the builders levelled the landscape. Then the late eighth-century complex was constructed; the church complex comprised three principal components: the church, atrium and baptistery. West of the church an enclosed cemetery was soon laid out, within which the excavators discovered rows of graves. Around the area to the south of the church a perimeter wall was erected a short time after the church was built. Neil Christie, in his report on the excavations (1991), proposes that this belonged to a fortification of the settlement in the period *c.* 815-50 as a result of the growing insecurity generated by the

Arab attacks on Rome and its region. Contemporary with this event was the laying of a trodden earth surface, almost certainly a courtyard level. Built up against the inner face of the perimeter wall was a large room *c.* 33 m long by 11 m wide, known as room 6, based upon a series of piers. The structure possessed a mortar floor. The basic design of this building is utilitarian, comprising a series of pier bases, which may have supported a roof sloping down from the perimeter wall. The excavators assumed that it had been partitioned into a number of smaller rooms. The simplicity of the plan, with one area being floored, suggests that it was part residence – perhaps for an agricultural supervisor (as in the case of the chamberlain's rooms in the collective workshop at San Vincenzo al Volturno, see below) – and part storehouse. Beyond this, in the south-east corner of the enclosure, lay a small room measuring 12 x 7 m. Built of stone with no definable floor, its function could not be determined. Similar stone buildings, less well preserved, were also found in this area, including room 1 with patches of opus sectile floor and room 2 with a re-used Roman threshold. Though the evidence is scanty, Neil Christie proposed that this complex of structures formed the administrative centre of the *domusculta*, and that areas provided for workshops, storage and for the accommodation of the estate workers lay close by.

Mola di Monte Gelato

One of the ninth-century dispersed estates of Santa Cornelia, known as Mola di Monte Gelato, has been found in the Treia valley, about 20 km to the north-east of Santa Cornelia. Excavations by the late Tim Potter have revealed a long occupation history spanning the first millennium. In sum, the site boasted a major Augustan courtyard villa situated on a terrace overlooking the river Treia; this was enlarged during the second century when a suite of baths was constructed beside the road leading to the villa. There followed an abandonment phase before in *c.* 350 a new complex was constructed with a small church. The complex certainly survived until the mid- to late sixth century, although by this late date timber partitions reveal a significant decline in investment in the structure. The church, it then appears, was renovated in the early ninth century with an associated baptistery, and alongside it a workshop housing a pottery kiln was constructed (Fig. 17). Close by, the long-abandoned second-century mausoleum was re-used as a habitation of some kind. A cave was also occupied at this time. In the tenth to eleventh centuries the church was enlarged with rooms flanking its north side. By 1053 the population had moved to the nearby hilltop site of Castellaccio, identifiable as castrum Capracorum from a papal bull of 1053.

The exceptionally fine excavations at Monte Gelato provide an important measure of the rhythms of rural settlement throughout the first millennium. The villa conforms to a pattern familiar throughout South Etruria. The very different character of the community that reoccupied the site *c.* AD 350 is manifested both by the architecture and by the finds. Although many old wall lines were followed, sometimes incorporating still-upstanding opus reticulatum from the Augustan villa, the new work was utilitarian in purpose and unostentious in design. Besides the living rooms, workshops and stores were gathered around the courtyard. The church was probably built around *c.* AD 400, leading the excavator to speculate that it was a papal estate as early as this. The excavator believes that the settlement was deserted by the seventh century, and speculates that its inhabitants might have moved up onto the hill known as Castellaccio (though no evidence was discovered to confirm this: Potter & King 1997: 426). The ninth-century successor complex as a result is seemingly puzzling. This was an elaborately decorated church with its adjoining baptistery, replete with sculpture of the type found at Santa Cornelia. However, apart

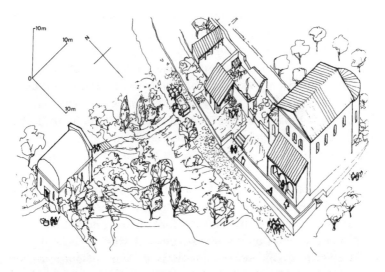

17. Reconstruction of the ninth-century nucleus at Mola di Monte Gelato (Latium).

from one workshop (housing a pottery kiln) and the re-used Roman features (the temple-tomb and rock-cut cave), other agrarian structures were absent. Nevertheless, as if to affirm its importance as a component of a *domusculta*, the products of the kiln were being distributed as far as Rome, where excavations at the Crypta Balbi have brought numerous examples to light.

The excavations produced little evidence of the later ninth or tenth century (Potter & King 1997: 426), as if to demonstrate that, with the Arab threat of the mid-ninth century, Santa Cornelia's fortunes had stalled, and consequently the sub-centre at Mola di Monte Gelato declined.

Continuity is absent at Santa Cornelia and misleading at Mola di Monte Gelato. These were later eighth-century settle-ments built where, presumably, some memory of Roman settlement existed. It would be misleading to suggest that either place simply sustained a classical system of dispersed farming beyond the sixth century; they did not. By the sixth century, if not before, settlement in both places was in decline. Two centuries later, perhaps some continuity of property bounds existed (as Wickham has suggested: 1979), but more than this is not borne out by the archaeological evidence. Indeed, it is tempting to interpret the *domuscultae* as part of a papal strategy to colonise deserted landscapes, much as was happening in Carolingian Austrasia at this time (cf. La Rocca 1998).

The *domusculta* of Santa Cornelia is particularly interesting because it appears to be a manor, similar in some ways to Santa Maria in Civita with the facilities for storage, and yet its form, with a church and baptistery, suggests it was at the hub of a constellation of sub-centres like Mola di Monte Gelato, where resources were first assembled, or in the case of pots, made, under the general supervision of the administrator of the *domusculta*. Santa Cornelia, then, was explicitly a papal manor that served as the centre for a community distributed over the Etrurian countryside where, in many parts as we have seen, peasants were already occupying hilltops (such as Mazzano Romano and Ponte Nepesino (cf. Potter & King 1997)). As a topographical form, much like Santa Maria in Civita, it appears to have failed during the mid-ninth century to be replaced by a more classical version of a manorial estate – that is, a hilltop village such as Castellaccio at Mola di Monte Gelato.

San Vincenzo al Volturno

The Benedictine monastery of San Vincenzo was founded in AD 703 beside the river Volturno in north-west Molise (Hodges 1997). Excavations at the site have shown conclusively that the early medieval settlement occupied the ruins of an late Roman estate centre, which in turn occupied parts of an earlier *vicus* dating back to later Samnite, republican and imperial times. The history of the settlement throws light on the villa-to-village debate.

The earliest nucleus at San Vincenzo was a Samnite community of unspecified dimensions situated on the east side of the river Volturno and its associated cemetery. This early community expanded during the republican period to occupy both sides of the river Volturno, reaching to the lowest flanks of Colle della Torre, a prominent hill on the west bank of the Volturno. A large ditch defined the southernmost extent of the eastern, original nucleus. Until the mid 1990s it was believed that the republican *vicus* was abandoned in the imperial age, when the *coloniae* of Aesernia and Venafrum were established some 20 km to the south, and a *villa rustica* was built beyond the limits of the old settlement (cf. Hodges 1997: 45-9). Further, it was believed, the villa was occupied until the end of the fourth century when it too was abandoned, in favour of a new, more defensive location on the flank of Colle della Torre (i.e. on the west bank of the river Volturno). Excavations on the east bank of the river Volturno in 1996-7, however, now indicate that this interpretation of the settlement sequence is no longer tenable (Gilkes & Moran 2001). Instead, it appears that the republican *vicus* probably shrank in size, but was sustained in a smaller form throughout the early and middle empire until *c.* AD 400. Limited excavations of the imperial villa suggest that it was a small *villa rustica*, somewhat smaller, for example, than the villa excavated in the neighbouring Biferno valley at Matrice (see Chapter 2). A shift in emphasis, it now appears, occurred in late antiquity, when the centre of this settlement was made in the form of a two- or three-floored tower – an unusual architectural form for the period – on a terrace on the west side of the river. Substantial occupation of the old nucleus (*vicus*) ceased, but more ephemeral, post-built buildings as well as structures, perhaps made of pisé, continued to occupy parts of the east bank. In short, the *vicus* had taken a new form, in a more defensive location, resembling the form described by Domenico Vera (1995) elsewhere it Italy, and now known from archaeological surveys on the Adriatic littoral in Abruzzo (Staffa 2000) and Apulia (Volpe 1998) (see Chapter 2). The later Roman centre, judging from the sample of burials found in the South Church (a cemetery church), was small but nevertheless amounted to as many as 40 persons made up of a number of families (cf. Hodges 1993).

The excavations suggest that the estate centre was largely or entirely deserted when the founding fathers of the monastery arrived at the beginning of the eighth century. The twelfth-century *Chronicon Vulturnense* describes its foundation as though it were in a primeval forest (cf. Le Goff 1988), even though the place was infused with a long history of occupation and, in Augé's sense, memory (1995). Had the occupants of the late Roman estate centre migrated to adjacent hilltops or indeed to nearby coastal centres? Judging from the survey by Staffa in the Abruzzo, we might favour either and indeed both explanations (Staffa 2000). What is clear is that the tower in the estate centre was demolished during the eighth century and its associated cemetery church was levelled before a new church, possibly the abbey-church of San Vincenzo Minore, was constructed by the monks. The new monastery, consistent with the period, was a small nucleus as opposed to a collection of units scattered around the side of Colle della Torre (see Chapter 3).

Great changes occurred at San Vincenzo as in similar monasteries elsewhere in Italy towards the end of the eighth century, as the impact of Charlemagne's influence in the peninsula was felt (cf. Cantino Wataghin 2000). Granted immunities and privileges by Charlemagne in AD 787, with resources garnered from its many new estates scattered across the south, a series of building campaigns led to a monastic city being constructed on the west bank around and on the slopes of Colle della Torre (Hodges 1997). The new monastery was essentially planned around an axial corridor – a sacred routeway connecting the old abbey-church, San Vincenzo Minore, to a new one, San Vincenzo Maggiore, consecrated in 808. As far as can be judged, the new plan was conceived as a number of modules, ranging from the claustrum on the river side, to collective workshops beyond (south of) the new abbey-church, and an enclosed church on the hilltop (cf. Hodges, Gibson & Mitchell 1997). Around this time, the new settlement for the servile dependants of the monastery, a *borgo*, expanded across the river, reoccupying the low-lying fields once the site of the Roman *villa rustica*. Here, separated from the monastic precinct, excavations brought to light traces of two areas of dense structures. One area, closer to the river Volturno, contained evidence of post-built and pisé buildings concerned with industrial activity including glass-working and pottery production (Gilkes & Moran 2001); the second area, set back from the river, comprised a large nucleus of post-built structures covering as much as two hectares (i.e. the area of the village of Poggibonsi), either dwellings for the monastic workforce or buildings used for storage.

It is perhaps tempting to interpret the ninth-century monastery as an urban phenomenon, taking many of its ideas from contemporary urban circumstances. This might be misleading. The intention may have been to create a city dedicated to God, but its component parts were drawn as much from the countryside as from the incipient towns of the age. To begin with the ritual elements of the monastery followed the Carolingian norms of the age. The craft workshops appear to be rural structures of a traditional kind that were modified for utilitarian purposes and, if anything, proved to be models for later urban shops such as those excavated in tenth-century Ferrara (cf. Gelichi 1997: 198-200). The *borgo*, with its mixture of pisé and post-built structures, appears to have comprised a variety

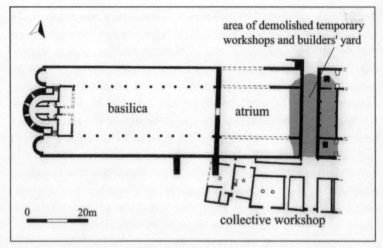

18. Plan of San Vincenzo Maggiore (Molise) in phase 5 (ninth century) showing the location of the collective workshop.

of rural building types known in antiquity and, as we have seen, in the early middle ages.

Particular attention should be paid to the collective workshop south of San Vincenzo Maggiore (Fig. 18). Its origins lay in a series of buildings serving the architects and craftsmen involved in the new abbey-church dating from *c.* 790-808. These temporary buildings were then remodelled as a linear workshop not unlike those found in late antique towns. These were dedicated to making enamels, glassware, fine metalwork, bonework and ivories – prestige goods that were probably used in transactions with patrons in the embryonic principality of Benevento. From our point of view, the significant phase in these workshops occurred after the earthquake of AD 848 severely damaged the monastery. Already suffering from the effects of the Beneventan civil unrest, the collective workshop was remodelled once more. Next to the metalsmith, a chamberlain's apartment was made. Next to this, a granary was made, similar in dimensions to the granary found at Montarrenti. Like the Montarrenti granary, this was burnt down, in this instance immediately before or during the Arab attack of 881. These excavations provide a small window on the changing axes of the monastery's external relations. While it flourished, it used prestige goods to acquire agrarian goods and services. Quite possibly the agrarian produce, being huge in quantity, was stored in the monastery's *borgo*. With the onset of civil strife, however, the monks needed to be more vigilant about controlling their foodstuffs, creating a storeroom next to the administrator. We can only assume that the administrator had an increasingly important role in managing the monastery's economy.

A survey of rural settlement in the upper Volturno valley showed a sharp decline in settlement after the third century, with nucleated centres such as San Vincenzo being sustained until the later fifth or sixth century. After this, it seems highly probable that there was a shift to hilltops. One possible site occupied at this time is Vacchereccia near San Vincenzo (see Chapter 3). Village formation in the *terra* of San Vincenzo, however, may have been stalled by the creation of the nucleated village forming part of the large ninth-century *borgo* at the monastery itself. In some respects the *vicus* of antiquity had been restored, albeit in a new guise. Not until the monastery was experiencing a recession in its fortunes in the mid-ninth century – or even later – is there any evidence of investment in the rural communities of the upper Volturno valley. First, churches were constructed at several key points in the valley in the 830s, one of which, at Colle Sant'Angelo, was excavated. Colle Sant'Angelo was small, grandly furnished with paintings and window glass, but nevertheless short-lived; by the tenth century it appears to have been demolished, in all probability its building materials being transported to the new *castello* of Colli a Volturno founded in AD 972. From this time, too, dates the small tower residence of Colle Castellano, described above.

In sum, in the early ninth century San Vincenzo became a massive manorial nucleus articulated around a new abbey-church, San Vincenzo Maggiore. Part of this nucleus was an associated *borgo* including craft-workshops and probable dwellings of a lay workforce, such as is described at St Denis in Paris and, closer to San Vincenzo, the suburb of Eulogimenopolis at Monte Cassino – an extramural settlement located far below the Benedictine monastery. In some ways, the monastery amounted to the nucleation of the *domusculta* of Santa Cornelia and all its dependent properties like Mola di Monte Gelato in one place. The new settlement must have had a huge impact upon the rural communities of the upper Volturno valley. Classic village life, such as we have described in Tuscany, for example, was probably delayed, as peasants sought opportunities in the monastery's *borgo*. Only with the mid-ninth-century recession did significant investment occur in rural society in the upper Volturno valley.

The tensions in the regional equilibrium came to a climax when an Arab band in collusion with the Bishop of Naples comprehensively sacked San Vincenzo on 10 October 881.

The subsequent history of San Vincenzo is inextricably entangled with the next steps in the process of village development. First, in the second half of the tenth century, it appears that the monastery invested in developing its properties in the upper Volturno – charters contained within the twelfth-century *Chronicon Vulturnense* register, a classic example of *incastellamento* (Wickham 1984). Second, drawing upon its new resources, during the first half of the eleventh century a nucleated Romanesque monastery was created within the ruins of the ninth-century monastic settlement. Third, late in the eleventh century, dissatisfied with this nucleus, the monks constructed a new community (the so-called New Abbey: Hodges 1997) within a ditched and fortified enclosure on the east side of the river Volturno, demolishing the old site to provide materials for the new buildings. Nearly twenty years of excavations have revealed a history that is far more complex in its regional and inter-regional rhythms than Mario del Treppo, the first historian of the monastery's estates, envisaged (1955). Like the *domusculta*, we have unearthed the rise and fall of an experiment in seigneurial control, located where a community had successfully existed more or less continuously since Iron Age times.

The introduction of *castelli*

Several generations after the insertion of the manor into nucleated ninth-century villages, local power became fully invested in aristocrats who defined the legal rights of their territories. Similarly, religious ritual became increasingly rooted in villages and needed its own local structure – the church. This was the product of a sea-change in political and social practice, as local lords or communities created rules for their own social group to compensate for the diminished public power of the state. *Incastellamento*, beginning in the mid- to later tenth century, is an expression of this transformation. It is a moment when villages were given foundation charters and, with these, a new status as *castelli*.

As we have noted throughout this book, for Pierre Toubert and his pupils, *incastellamento* in the tenth and eleventh centuries marked a rupture with the past. Toubert argued that a proliferation of local aristocracies gave rise to the need to control their human and landed resources more effectively in nucleated villages. There is little doubting the physical impact of this process; it is the genesis of the process itself which is at the heart of our debate. Without doubt, excavations throughout Italy have affirmed that it was a highly significant episode. Nonetheless, it is our contention that only by comprehending the origins of local power, and, in particular, the evolution of all

19. Reconstruction drawing of Rocca San Silvestro (Tuscany) in the twelfth to thirteenth centuries.

the elements such as stone fortifications and dwellings associated with the proliferation of local power from the later tenth century onwards, that we can appreciate the particular significance of the *castelli* that continue to characterise the Italian countryside.

Rocca San Silvestro, the mining village in western Tuscany, is a good example of *incastellamento* in Toubert's sense (Fig. 19). This conical-shaped hill, located in an area where metal extraction had been taking place since Etruscan times, was not occupied until the later tenth century. No traces of post-built seventh- to ninth-century structures were found here. Instead it was envisaged as a seigneurial village from its outset, with a small castle, a *rocca*, on the apex of the cone, and a church set onto a ledge below. Around the girth of the hill, rings of dwellings were constructed (Francovich 1991; Francovich & Wickham 1994). Bianchi has shown that the first dwellings were constructed by the peasants themselves. Shortly afterwards, however, in the eleventh to early twelfth centuries, the dwellings were completely remodelled, displaying considerable quality in their construction. Bianchi argues that the Della Gherardesca family were offering incentives to the peasantry, providing knowledge about stone construction, which would entice them to stay and work on the estate (1995: 377). The same picture was observed at Montarrenti in a somewhat poorer locality. The first phase of the *castello* belonging to the tenth to eleventh centuries is characterised by four large timber buildings occupying Area 1000 on the summit (previously the site of the granary). This was followed at the beginning of the twelfth century by a radical transformation of the entire site. A new walled enclosure was built around the summit within which two towers and a grand *palatium* were erected. These tower-houses probably imitated aristocratic dwellings in nearby Siena. Significantly, as at Rocca San Silvestro, the ring of peasant dwellings around the midslope were rebuilt in fine, worked stone, resulting in dwellings which resemble manor-houses in twelfth-century England.

Not all villages were as successful, or indeed prosperous. The little village of Vetrana, overlooking the Biferno valley in Molise, lasted only two centuries, and while it boasted a stone church, its peasant dwellings were of rubble (cf. Hodges & Wickham 1995). At Colle Castellano in the *terra* of San Vincenzo al Volturno, the enclosure wall erected in the central decades of the tenth century to establish the *castellum* involved demolishing the earlier stone tower, described above. The huge wall was made with hard concrete, but inside it only traces of post-built structures were discovered. The attractive terms offered to peasants in order to lure them to this village (Wickham 1984) were evidently enhanced by the prominent sense of security and status that the new walls lent to the place. Curiously, it was to be almost another century before the owners of the estate, the monastery of San Vincenzo al Volturno, enclosed the abbey complex (see above).

Incastellamento has attracted studies of villages in every region of Italy. From the Alps to Sicily, excavations have illuminated the explosion of villages and the rhythms of peasant living. Without doubt, many villages were new creations, born of the sharp growth in the economy of the Italian states as Mediterranean commerce was revived and flourished. Hence, it has not been difficult for Toubert's pupils to discover villages in the Sabine Hills – in the territory of Farfa – that were created for the first time in the eleventh or twelfth century (cf. Hubert 2000). Nor should we ignore the fact that some earlier villages, such as Poggibonsi, failed at this time. However, while *incastellamento* provided a new authority for local lords, our thesis is that this had grown out of a dialectical relationship with the peasantry that owed its origins to village living as far back as late antiquity.

Conclusions

There has been a strong temptation to regard Italy as separated from the rhythms and trends of north-west Europe in the Middle Ages (cf. La Rocca 1998). As McCormick points out in the quotation cited at the beginning of this chapter, the later eighth and ninth centuries were a period of great openness (2001). Besides Frankish armies, a great many pilgrims and travellers criss-crossed Italy en route from England or the Frankish kingdoms to the Holy Land. We underestimate the exchange of ideas and information at our peril. This surely is the context for the *curtis*. It is a form that is well known from the ninth-century Frankish *Capitularis de Villis*; it is also known from excavations as diverse as the grand complex at Tilleda (cf. Galetti 2001: 74-9) and the modest south German versions at Barbing-Kreuzhof (Stadt Regensburg) – a solitary manor with service buildings and a church, and Lauchheim-Mittelhofen (near Stuttgart) with one large farm surrounded by several small ones, come to mind (Bücker & Hoeper 1999). The sources lay emphasis upon the storage capacity of the *curtis*, as a point of accumulation and administration. The longhouse complex at Poggibonsi surely meets this description, as do the storage and production facilities of Santa Cornelia and San Vincenzo al Volturno, as indeed, for that matter, do the grain storage pits excavated at Santa Maria in Civita and at Lanciano (Staffa 1994: fig. 72). The settlement form was evidently a critical feature of the transformation of the Italian countryside. In architectural terms, Wickham has argued that stone-built rural manor-houses like Santa Cornelia were modelled upon urban buildings (1999), yet, we should note, Meneghini and Santangeli Valenzani (2001: 26) in their report on the stone-built ninth-century aristocratic residence found in the Forum of Nerva at Rome liken it to a rural *curtis*. As yet the evidence is too slight, but the issue is undoubtedly intriguing and encourages us to consider, at least, whether towns with a tradition of timber buildings from the fifth to the ninth centuries had in fact adopted a rural rhythm of construction (cf. Brogiolo & Gelichi 1997: 131-5; 146-50). Without doubt, in the process of finding a dialectical accord with a peasantry which had been largely untroubled by services and taxes since late antiquity, architectural form was important. Enclosure walls, we postulate, were significant in overcoming lingering doubts about the radical social change inherent in the legal implications of *incastellamento*.

Mentioned first in eighth-century documents, the *curtis* has been interpreted by historians as the first step in a process of re-organisation of landed lordship represented archaeologically by the castle. But the *curtis* was essentially a system of relationships between private individuals, based upon a strict social hierarchy. It is thus difficult to believe that estate centres could only have been made up of one or a few isolated houses, of which almost no archaeological traces remain. We have argued that it is more likely that the estate centres were located in centralised hilltop sites, of which some clear cut material traces survive. In these centres, after an initial, broadly egalitarian phase there followed a phase of distinct social division, a chronology reflected in the written sources. This is proof that the aristocratic classes of the late Lombard period, but especially the later eighth- and ninth-century Carolingian period, had started a process of reorganisation of the landed property and, concomitantly, a greater hierarchy of power and authority. The final stage in the protracted process of landscape formation is the *castello*, the seigneurial castle. Replacing the earlier lordly *curtis*, a new, more exacting authority was superimposed upon a variety of settlement types, both consolidating existing forms and, as in the classic case of the new mining village of Rocca San Silvestro in western Tuscany, in areas unoccupied since antiquity.

Between the eighth and ninth centuries, the Italian countryside was affected by processes of reaggregation of the population and the redefinition of the settlement network. The relations between the system of churches and monasteries on the one hand, and the world of hilltop villages on the other, may be perceived in dialectical terms. In the former, there prevailed an ancient model: around the religious centre arose a small scattered settlement destined to grow; in the latter, social relations within the village communities were redefined, involving a definitive break with the past. For some centuries these two models confronted one another, but the fact that as early as the tenth century many large monasteries were already starting to decline, and that churches were brought within the newly created castles (*castelli*), and not vice versa, indicates how profitable the investment by landed lords in hilltop sites had been. It is tempting to conclude that the monastic city with its

4. *From Curtis to Castello*

borgo, like the *domusculta*, was an aberrant settlement form of a proto-feudal age, when the élite, conscious of the classical past, were striving to make a new imprint upon their landscapes.

5

Conclusions: Four Stages
of Transformation

When the learned men of the Carolingian age drew up
estate records, representing their society as stable and
unchanging, this was most likely the outcome of a long-
term process of interpretation and negotiation, with the
landscape as its main source. It is difficult to gain a clear
idea of these matters, for this was a dialectical process in
which different actors had different voices. Just as the
audience of a dominant representation of power was diverse, so too were the interpretations, as well as the
processes of negotiation between different groups about
power and the basic values and ideas in society. Because
spatial elements, or the landscape as a whole, had such a
wide audience, there are considerable opportunities for
archaeologists to contribute to the debate on the constitution of society. Our greatest challenge is to develop our
discipline in such a way that we can explain not just the
practices of different groups, but the interaction between
dominant representations and dominant interpretations
as well. (Theuws 2001: 216)

It is tempting to picture the Middle Ages as simple and static.
Nothing is farther from the truth. The archaeology of late
antique and early medieval Italy reveals a history made all the
more complex by the three ecological zones of the landscape – a

coastal littoral, deep inland valleys, and watersheds and high mountains – as well as the ever-changing political geography of the peninsula. Obviously, in a discipline that has effectively been active for little more than a quarter-century, it would be wise to be cautious about the material evidence until more case-studies are at our disposal. Nonetheless, the archaeological evidence provides a picture of the transformation of the countryside between late antiquity and the early middle ages, shedding fresh light upon the historical debate about rural sociology of this formative period.

Towards a new rural sociology for early medieval Italy

First of all, the landscapes of late antiquity underwent a dramatic phase of decline between the third and fourth centuries. In the fourth century, coinciding with the Constantinian revival, numerous rural sites were remodelled throughout Italy, sometimes, as in the case of San Giovanni di Ruoti, with prominent architectural features. Commonly the internal arrangements of old buildings were extensively altered with new, seemingly makeshift partition walls. These new country houses lasted barely a century before, in the Theodosian period, shorn of economic support, they were steadily abandoned. One consequence that is becoming apparent is that, notwithstanding the demise of the Constantinian villas in the course of the fifth century, their landscapes were sustained in one form or another up until the time of the Gothic war in central decades of the sixth century. It is now generally believed that the Gothic war favoured the rise of a new military élite, not only in Lombard areas but also in Byzantine territories. One marked outcome of this was the virtual demise of the traditional rural aristocracy.

The definitive dissolution of ancient landscapes and the beginnings of nucleated hilltop settlements began in the seventh century. The new settlements evolved largely thanks to the peasant population and without any real obstacles. As we have shown, the notion of hilltop living spread rapidly throughout many regions in the peninsula, constituting the first phase of landscapes that have evolved largely unchanged up until modern times. The second phase, in the later eighth or ninth century, is marked by the presence of a new rural élite whose seigneurial dwellings, like the concomitant new forms of agricultural management, mark a significant step in the transformation towards the familiar medieval countryside. In the past historians have tended to emphasise the part played by dispersed settlements as the link between antiquity and the middle ages. New archaeological evidence from sites such as Montarrenti, Poggibonsi and Scarlino casts doubt on this. Villages, we have argued, provided the matrix of rural society from the seventh century onwards, and not surprisingly were the points in the landscape in which the new rural aristocracy of the Carolingian age invested. With ever-weakening state power in the later ninth and tenth centuries, as many historians have convincingly shown, the embryonic rural aristocracy established itself as an effective alternative. In the written sources, this moment is reflected in terms of new village foundation-charters; in the material record, the most prominent manifestations are the new fortifications created as the lord exhibited his jurisdiction over his territory.

In describing our perspective of the debate about the transition from Roman villas to hilltop villages we have identified four stages. These are:

(1) New villas and villages (*vici*) took shape after the Constantinian reforms. Places such as the village replacing the villa at Torrita di Siena in Tuscany were prototypes of a medieval settlement form. In some cases the lord's residence is clearly

denoted, as in the tower at San Vincenzo al Volturno, but in many cases the new sub-division of rooms within existing villa mansions or even the simple accommodation within the Gothic palace at Monte Barro reveal changing standards. All the evidence points to the large-scale desertion of the countryside by the aristocracy on the one hand, and, where the rural élite remained in residence, they lived in an economic and social context which was increasingly regional in character and remote from centres of government. Hence, a villa such as that at San Giovanni di Ruoti almost certainly functioned within a Basilicatan environment; its fine mosaic belonged to a highly provincial culture while its pig-production was destined for local consumption as opposed to reinforce Rome's needs for cheap meat, as was once believed. Into this flagging, increasingly regionalised economy ventured small immigrant groups, who, seeking to enjoy the benefits of the first world, invariably engaged it with new energy (cf. Härke 1997).

(2) The political crises of the sixth and earlier seventh centuries constituted a final rupture with the classical past. Public power had been largely overthrown. The crisis was perhaps slower in Byzantine Italy, where Mediterranean exchange continued substantially longer in urban centres such as Rome, Naples and Otranto. Artisan skills accordingly became rarer, trade-routes were less travelled – changes manifest in the desolate levels of material culture that appear in the archaeological record (cf. McCormick 2001; Ward-Perkins 2001). The Lombard aristocracy, influenced by the urban values of late Roman Italy, occupied decaying urban centres (admirably revealed in Brescia, for example: Brogiolo and Gelichi 1997) rather than their traditional rural homesteads. Local aristocracies, some with roots in the pre-Roman period, began to exert limited influence over small territories, such as has been suggested for the Volterra district of Tuscany (Augenti & Terrenato 2000). Given these

circumstances, this must have been the golden age of a largely independent peasantry (cf. Wickham 1999: 19; Wickham 1989: 149). (Carandini, it should be recorded, contests this as a false view of this distressing age, drawing upon the treatment of the peasantry in Soviet Russia to challenge Wickham: Carandini 1993: 25 and n. 19.) Nonetheless, throughout Italy the peasantry, in search of more effective ecological niches, abandoned classical estate centres almost certainly to create new farming collectives – villages (see, for example, the village of Gorfigliano above Lucca in Tuscany where the villagers occupied an upland niche based upon exploiting the chestnuts: Quirós Castillo, Gobbato, Giovannetti and Sorrentino 2000). The seventh-century hilltop settlements of Poggibonsi in Tuscany and Casale San Donato in Latium show that considerable variability existed in the size and material conditions of these new places. Hilltop living begs many questions. Were these new places devoid of memory: non-places in Marc Augé's sense (1995)? Quite the contrary, it now seems: many of the chosen hilltops had been occupied in Iron Age or earlier prehistoric times, but is it conceivable that some collective memory of such origins still existed in the sixth or seventh century? Was the peasantry, like the brethren of the new monasteries, seeking new homes in the 'desert-forest' (cf. Le Goff 1988), joining in communion with the natural order of things? Certainly the sociological motives underlying this significant shift in the history of settlement in Italy merits careful reconsideration. A recent study fuels this picture of a bucolic age: Giovannini contends that the death-rate of small children up to the age of five was no more than 30%, and that 15-20% of the adult population lived past 50 years of age. 'In fact the average rural peasant of the sixth-seventh century had the strong opinion that it was certainly to his advantage to bear fewer children' (2001: 112). The impoverished circumstances of the late republic and early empire were a distant memory.

5. Conclusions: Four Stages of Transformation

(3) The threshold of change occurred with the advent of Carolingian interest in Italy. As Wickham cogently puts it: 'It was 800, not 1000, that was in most parts of Carolingian Europe the turning-point for the establishment of local aristocratic dominance. After that, all dissension was between landed political élites: greater versus lesser lords; aristocrats legitimised by public office versus those without; and not least, clerics versus laity. Faced with competing dominators, peasants will have looked for the lesser evil in every case; who that lesser evil actually was will of course have been different from village to village' (Wickham 1997: 198). After the 770s new agrarian and ideological institutions were created in the countryside. These new institutional structures ranged from new estate centres as diverse as that imposed within the hilltop village of Poggibonsi and the papal farm of Santa Cornelia. Quite clearly the so-called *curtis* took many different forms, invariably being a manorial initiative within pre-existing villages. From this moment stems productive specialisation, illustrated most emphatically by the workshops and the associated *borgo* belonging to the Benedictine monastery of San Vincenzo al Volturno in Molise. This specialisation points to the beginnings of an interlocking system for individual and social needs that necessitated the organisation of rights and obligations. The Carolingian premise of divided labour had taken root and in short, rural Italy was experiencing the beginnings of a social revolution that led inevitably to the diminution of peasant rights. Wickham counsels against over-emphasising the authority exercised by local lords: 'the lords instead were dominating the field of exchange' (2000: 33). This interpretation holds true for great centres like Monte Cassino, the churches of Rome and San Vincenzo al Volturno (cf. Hodges 1997), but not for the seigneurial homes of coastal villages like Scarlino (Tuscany) where imports are absent. As we have seen, even the hilltop *curtis* at Santa Maria in Civita (Molise), located near the Adria-

111

tic sea, while rich in a mixture of cereals and evidently well-supplied with pots from a regional centre, only boasted a few glass sherds, a fragment of soapstone and a quernstone that had come from further afield (Hodges, Barker & Wade 1980).

(4) The next step in modern Italian history occurred in the tenth century. However, the archaeological evidence now indicates that this was not the revolution in rural sociology that it was once thought to be. Clearly, several generations after the insertion of the manor into nucleated ninth-century villages, local power was now fully invested in aristocrats who defined the legal rights of their territories. Villages needed, and began to gain more government. Similarly, religious ritual became increasingly rooted in villages and needed its own local structures – the parish. These were the products of a sea-change in political and social practice as local lords or communities created rules for their own social group to compensate for the diminished public power of the state. *Incastellamento* in the mid- to later tenth century is an expression of this transformation. This expression was based upon four centuries of village life, when networks of new villages were founded and landlords explicitly promoted the clearance and colonisation of lands that had been abandoned since the third or fourth century. This coincided with the establishment of rural markets on the eve of the revival of the Mediterranean economy. What were the advantages to the peasantry of entering into these agreements? Why should they produce for lords who might sell this produce in the new markets? The archaeology provides a transparently clear answer. Every village was now fully locked into an interdependent system in which the peer-pressure of material benefits was too great to ignore. Knowledge of good construction techniques leading to stone-built peasant houses of high quality was widely available by the eleventh century (Bianchi 1995: 377). Large quantities of pottery and prolific amounts of faunal remains

5. Conclusions: Four Stages of Transformation

from villages such as Colle Castellano (Molise) and Montarrenti (Tuscany) also paint a vivid picture of the moment of
change. Hence, a modest village such as Vacchereccia in upland
Molise obtained volcanic-tempered wares from the Bay of
Naples and 1% of its wares were glazed. The contrast with the
materially impoverished circumstances of the seventh and
eighth centuries could not be clearer.

Future directions

We have two particular thoughts about this debate, looking to
the future.

(1) The future role of the medieval historian. The import of this
book, drawing upon recent archaeological research, contends
that some historians have been transfixed by the year 1000, the
concept of feudalism which furnishes them with rich bodies of
written sources, and the shadow of great interpreters such as
Marc Bloch and Georges Duby. As Chris Wickham puts it: 'Focus
on the year 1000 and its associated transformation gains at its
edge in France from its role in French imageries of national
centrality ....The French often seem to see the decentralized
feudal world as the moment of opportunity in central medieval
Europe' (Wickham 1997: 199-200). Clearly the issue is not a
trivial one, and not a 'nuanced observation', as Bisson dismis-
sively suggests (1997: 222). At the same time, seduced by the
intellectually fascinating and elegant writings of historians
such as Peter Brown, and affirmed by the episodic production
and near ubiquitous distribution of type fossils like African Red
Slip ware, archaeologists have pushed the transformation of the
Roman world well into the seventh century, leaving only a brief
period of a century or so to be bridged until the Carolingian
revival. Today this overview merits serious deconstructing.
More specifically, challenging the Toubert model described in

113

Chapter 1, we have attempted to illustrate the inherent importance of the archaeological evidence for constructing a historical
model which, as it happens, calls into question the purpose and
character of the written sources, and necessarily causes us to
examine how and why certain text-based histories are made.

(2) Future archaeological research. The rupture between late
antiquity and the early middle ages should encourage archaeologists and historians to be fascinated by the final episodes of
the classical settlement system. Beyond doubt, the post-built
structures marking the final phase of great villas such as San
Giusto in Apulia (Volpe 1998) or Settefinestre in Tuscany
(Carandini 1985: 92) are of supreme interest. Let us not be
seduced by Victorian images of dreamy shepherds camping in
these ruins. Plainly, good quality stratigraphic excavations have
indicated that these vestigial last phases of villa occupation are
in fact harbingers of a settlement form soon to be imprinted
upon hilltops. If we wish to understand the changing rhythms
of the second half of the first millennium – and in particular
whether there was a demographic collapse at this time – it is
essential, too, to document the first stages of the medieval
village in greater detail. To do this effectively, more large-scale
excavations are needed of the first phases of those settlements
which proved to be successful during the central and later
centuries of the middle ages. Excavations such as those at
Montarrenti in Tuscany, a village still occupied to this day,
however complex and logistically complicated, offer new texts –
and most of all a bridge between the Object and the Word, as
Moreland has put it (2001a) – for understanding this critical
period in Italian and European history.

Bibliography

Andreolli, B. & Montanari, M. (1983) *L'azienda curtense in Italia: proprietà della terra e lavoro contadino nei secoli VIII-XI*, Bologna, Editrice CLUEB.

Arthur, P. (1988) 'La perdita dell'innocenza', *Archeologia in Campagna* 1: 107-11.

Ascheri, M. & Kurze, W. (eds) (1989) *L'Amiata nel medioevo*, Rome, Viella.

Augé, M. (1995) *Non-Places: Introduction to an Anthropology of Supermodernity* (trans. Amy Jacobs), London, Verso.

Augenti, A. & Terrenato, N. (2000) 'Le sedi dei potere nel territorio di Volterra: una lunga prospettiva (secoli VIIa.C. – XIII d.C.)', in G-P. Brogiolo (ed.) *Il Congresso Nazionale di Archeologia Medievale*, Florence, All'Insegna del Giglio: 298-303.

Balzaretti, R. (1992) 'The creation of Europe', *History Workshop Journal* 33: 181-96.

Barker, G. (1991) 'Approaches to archaeology survey', in G. Barker & J. Lloyd (eds) *Roman Landscapes*, London, British School at Rome: 1-9.

—— (1995) *A Mediterranean Valley: Landscape Archaeology and Annales History in the Biferno Valley*, London, Leicester University Press.

Bianchi, G. (1995) 'L'analisi dell'evoluzione di un sapere technico per una rinnovata interpretazione dell'assetto abitativo e delle strutture edilizie del villaggio fortificato di Rocca San Silvestro', in E. Boldrini & R. Francovich (eds) *Acculturazione e mutamenti: prospettive nell archeologia medievale del Mediterraneo*, Florence, All'Insegna del Giglio: 361-96.

Bisson, T.N. (1994) 'The feudal revolution', *Past and Present* 142: 6-42.

—— (1997) Reply, *Past and Present* 155: 208-25.

Bowden, W. & Hodges, R. (forthcoming) 'Balkan ghosts? Nationalism and the question of rural continuity in Albania', in N. Christie & S. Scott (eds) *Landscapes of Change: The Evolution of the Countryside from Late Antiquity to the Early Middle Ages*, Aldershot, Scolar Press.

Bowes, K. & Hodges, R. (2002) 'Santa Maria in Civita revisited', *Papers of the British School at Rome* 70: 359-61.

Breda, A. & Brogiolo, G.P. (1985) 'Piadena, loc. Castello 1984. Lotti 2 e 3', *Archeologia Medievale* XII: 181-8.

Brogiolo, G.P. (1994) 'Edilizia residenziale in Lombardia (V-VIII secolo)', in G.P. Brogiolo (ed.) *Edilizia residenziale tra V e VIII secolo,* Mantua, Società Archeologica Padana: 102-14.

—— (1996a) *La fine delle ville romane: trasformazioni nelle campagne tra tarda antichità e alto medioevo*, Mantua, Società Archeologica Padana.

—— (1996b) 'Conclusioni', in Broglio (1996a): 107-10.

—— (2000) 'Towns, forts and countryside: archaeological models for northern Italy and the early Lombard period (AD 568-650)', in G.P. Brogiolo *et al.* (eds) *Towns and their Territories between Late Antiquity and the Early Middle Ages,* Leiden, Brill: 299-324.

—— (2001) (ed.) 'Luoghi di culto tra VII e VIII secolo', in G.P. Brogiolo (ed.), *Le chiese rurali tra VII e VIII secolo in Italia Settentrionale,* Mantua, Società Archeologica Padana: 199-203.

—— & Castelletti, L. (eds) (1991) *Archeologia a Monte Barro: il grande edificio e le torri,* Lecco, Stefanoni.

—— & Gelichi, S. (1997) *La città nell'alto medioevo italiano*, Rome, Laterza.

Brown, E. (1974) 'The tyranny of a construct: feudalism and historians of medieval Europe', *American History Review* 79: 1063-88.

Brown, P. (1971) *The World of Late Antiquity AD 150-750*, London, Thames & Hudson.

—— (2002) *Poverty and Leadership in the Later Roman Empire*, Hanover, University of New Hampshire Press.

Brown, T. (1978) 'Settlement and military policy in Byzantine Italy', in H. McK. Blake, T. Potter & D.B. Whitehouse (eds) *Papers in Italian Archaeology I*, Oxford, British Archaeological Reports, International Series 41: 323-38.

—— (1984) *Officers and Gentlemen: Imperial Administration and Aristocratic Power in Byzantine Italy, AD 554-800*, London, British School at Rome.

Bücker, C. & Hoeper, M. (1999) 'First aspects of social hierarchy of settlements in Merovingian southwest Germany', in C. Fabech & J. Ringtved (eds) *Settlement and Landscape: Proceedings of a Conference in Århus, Denmark, May 4-7 1998*, Moesgård, Jutland Archaeological Society: 441-54.

Cambi, F. (1996) *Carta archeologica della Provincia di Siena: Il Monte Amiata*, vol. 2, Siena, Nuova Immagine.

—— & Mascione, C. (1998) 'Ceramiche tardoantiche da Torrita di

Bibliography

Siena', in L. Saguì (ed.) *Ceramica in Italia: VI-VII secolo. Atti del convegno in onore di J.W. Hayes*, Florence, All'Insegna del Giglio: 629-34.

Cantini, F. (2003) *Lo scavo archeologico del castello di Montarrenti (Siena). Per la storia della formazione del villaggio medievale in Toscana (secc. VII-XV)*, Florence, All'Insegna del Giglio.

Cantino Wataghin, G. (1994) 'Il territorio', in R. Francovich & G. Noyé (eds) *La storia dell'alto medioevo italiano all luce dell'archaeologia*, Florence, All'Insegna del Giglio: 142-50.

—— (2000) 'Monasteri tra VIII e IX secolo: evidenze archeologiche per l'Italia settentrionale,' in C. Bertelli & G.P. Brogiolo (eds) *Il futuro dei Longobardi: l'Italia e la costruzione dell'Europa di Carlo Magno*, Milan, Skira: 129-42.

Carandini, A. (1985) *Settefinestre: una villa schiavistica nell' Etruria Romana*, vol. 2: *La Villa nelle sue parti*, Modena, Panini.

—— (1993) 'L'ultima civiltà sepolta o del massimo oggetto desueto, secondo un archeologo', in A. Carandini (ed.) *Storia di Roma. 3 L'Età Tardoantica. II I Loughi e Le Culture*, Turin, Einaudi: 11-38.

—— & Cambi, F. (with Celuzza, M. & Fentress, E.) (2002) *Paesaggi d'Etruria. Valle dell'Albegna, Valle d'Oro, Valle del Chiarone, Valle del Tafone*, Rome, Edizioni di Storia e Letteratura.

Carocci, S. (1998) 'Signori, castelli, feudi', in C. Fumian (ed.) *Storia medievale*, Rome, Donzelli: 247-67

Carver, M. (1993) *Arguments in Stone*, Oxford, Oxbow Books.

Chapelot, J. (1993) 'L'habitat rural: organisation et nature', *L'Ile de France de Clovis à Hugues Capet*, Paris, Musée Archéologique Départemental du Val-d'Oise: 178-99.

—— & Fossier, R. (1980) *Le village et la maison au moyen âge*, Paris, Hachette.

Christie, N. (ed.) (1991) *Three South Etrurian churches*, London, British School at Rome.

—— (1993) *The Lombards*, Oxford, Blackwell.

Citter, C. (1997) 'I doni funebri nella Toscana longobarda ed il loro inquadramento nelle vicende storico-archeologiche del popolamento', in L. Paroli (ed.) *L'Italia centro settentrionale in età longobarda*, Florence, All'Insegna del Giglio: 185-211.

Comba, R & Settia, A (1984) *Castelli: storia e archeologia*, Turin, Comune di Cuneo.

D'Angela, C. & Volpe, G. (1994) 'Aspetti storici e archeologici dell'alto medioevo in Puglia', in R. Francovich & G. Noyé (eds) *La storia dell'altomedioevo italiano alla luce dell'archeologia*, Florence, All'Insegna del Giglio: 361-78.

Delogu, P. (1988) 'Tavola rotonda', in Francovich & Milanese (1988): 267-75.

—— (1994) *Introduzione alla Storia Medievale*, Rome, Carocci.

117

———— (1998) 'Reading Pirenne again', in R. Hodges & W. Bowden (eds), *The Sixth Century: Production, Distribution and Demand,* Leiden, Brill: 15-40.

Del Treppo, M. (1955) 'Vita economica e sociale in una grande abbazia del Mezzogiorno: San Vincenzo al Volturno', *Archivio storico per le province napoletane* 35: 31-110.

Duchesne, L. (1886) (ed.) *Liber Pontificalis,* Paris/Rome.

Dunbabbin, K.M.D. (1983) 'The San Giovanni mosaic in the context of late Roman mosaic production in Italy', in M. Gualtieri, M. Salvatore & A. Small (eds) *Lo scavo di S. Giovanni di Ruoti ed il periodo tardoantico in Basilicata,* Bari, Adriatica editrice: 47-57.

Ellis, S. (1988) 'The end of the Roman house', *American Journal of Archaeology* 92: 565-76.

Ellis, R. (1993) 'Power, architecture and décor: how the late Roman aristocrat appeared to his guests', in E.K. Gazda (ed.), *Roman Art in the Private Sphere,* Ann Arbor, University of Michigan Press: 117-56.

Emerick, J. (1998) *The Tempietto del Clitunno near Spoleto,* Philadelphia, Penn State Press.

Feller, L. (1998) *Les Abruzzes médiévales: territoire, économie et société en Italie centrale du IXe au XIIe siècle,* Rome, École Française de Rome.

Fentress, L. & Cambi, F. (1989) 'Villas to castles: first millennium AD. Demography in the Albegna Valley', in K. Randsborg (ed.) *The Birth of Europe,* Rome, Danish Institute in Rome: 74-86.

———— & Perkins P. (1989) 'Counting African Red Slip Ware', *L'Africa Romana* 5: 205-14.

Finley, M.I. (1977) 'The ancient city: from Fustel de Coulanges to Max Weber and beyond', *Comparative Studies in Society and History* 19: 305-27.

Fiocchi Nicolai, V. (1994) Discussione, in R. Francovich & G. Noyé (eds), *La storia dell'alto medioevo italiano alla luce dell'archeologia,* Florence, All'Insegna del Giglio: 403-6.

Fossier, R. (1982) *Enfance de l'Europe. Xe – XIIe siècles. Aspects économiques et sociaux. L'homme et son espace,* Paris, PUF.

Francovich, R. (ed.) (1985) *Scarlino I, Storia e territorio,* Florence, All'Insegna del Giglio.

———— (1991) *Rocca San Silvestro,* Rome, Leonardo-De Luca.

———— & Ginatempo, M. (2000) 'Introduzione', in R. Francovich & M. Ginatempo (eds) *Castelli. Storia e archeologia del potere nella Toscana medievale,* vol. 1, Florence, All' Insegna del Giglio: 7-24.

———— & Hodges, R. (1989) 'Archeologia e storia del villaggio fortificato di Montarrenti (Si): un caso o un modello?' in R. Francovich & M. Milanese (eds) 'Lo scavo archeologico di Montarrenti e i problemi

Bibliography

dell'incastellamento medievale. Esperienze a confronto', *Archeologia medievale* XVI: 15-38

—— & Milanese, M. (1988) *Lo scavo archeologico di Montarrenti e i problemi dell'incastellamento medievale*, Florence, Università di Siena.

—— & Wickham, C. (1994) 'Uno scavo archeologico e il problema dello sviluppo della Signoria territoriale: Rocca San Silvestro e i rapporti di produzione minerari', *Archeologia Medievale* XXI: 7-30.

Fumagalli, V. (1987) *Quando il cielo s'oscura*, Bologna, Il Mulino.

Galetti, P. (2001) *Uomini e case nel medioevo tra occidente e oriente*, Rome, Laterza.

Gatier, P-L. (1995) 'Villages du Proche Orient protobyzantine (4ème – 7ème s.). Étude régionale', in G.R.D. King & A. Cameron (eds) *The Byzantine and Early Islamic Near East 2: Land Use and Settlement Patterns*, Princeton, Darwin Press: 17-48.

Gazzetti, G. (1995) 'La villa romana in località Selvicciola (Ischia di Castro – VT)', in N. Christie (ed.) *Settlement and Economy in Italy 1500 BC to AD 1500. Papers of the 5th conference of Italian archeology*, Oxford, BAR International Series: 297-302.

—— & Zifferero, A. (eds) (1990) 'Progetto Monti della Tolfa – Valle del Mignone: secondo rapporto di attività (1985-1989)', *Archaeologia Medievale* XVII: 435-76.

Gelichi, S. (1997) *Introduzione all' Archeologia Medievale*, Rome, La Nuova Italia Scientifica.

Gilkes, O. & Moran, M. (2001) 'San Vincenzo without walls – excavations 1996-7', *Papers of the British School at Rome* 59: 385-92.

Ginatempo, M. & Giorgi, A. (2000) 'Documentary sources for the history of medieval settlements in Tuscany', in J. Bintliff & K. Sbonias (eds) *Reconstructing Past Population Trends in Mediterranean Europe*, Oxford, Oxbow Books: 173-93.

Giovannini, F. (2001) *Natalità, mortalità e demografia dell'Italia medievale sulla base dei dati archeologici*, Oxford, BAR International Series: 950.

Grassi, M.T. (1988) 'Rinvenimenti monetali da Angera (Varese). Scavi 1980-1984', *Bollettino di Numismatica*, 11: 7-151.

Härke, H. (1997) 'Archaeologists and migrations: a problem of attitude?', *Current Anthropology* 38: 1-32.

Hayes, J.W. (1972) *Late Roman Pottery*, London, British School at Rome.

—— (1998) 'The study of Roman pottery in the Mediterranean: 23 years after *Late Roman Pottery*', in Saguì (1998): 9-17.

Hodges, R. (1989) *The Anglo-Saxon Achievement*, London, Duckworth.

—— (1993) (ed.) *San Vincenzo al Volturno, 1: the 1980-86 excavations*, London, British School at Rome.

Bibliography

———— (1995) (ed.) *San Vincenzo al Volturno, 2: the 1980-86 excavations,* London, British School at Rome.

———— (1997) *Light in the Dark Ages: The Rise and Fall of San Vincenzo al Volturno,* London: Duckworth.

———— & Rovelli, A. (1998) 'San Vincenzo in the sixth century', *Papers of the British School at Rome* 66: 245-6.

———— & Whitehouse, D. (1983) *Mohammed, Charlemagne and the Origins of Europe,* London, Duckworth.

———— & Wickham, C. (1995) 'The evolution of hilltop villages (AD 600-1500)', in G. Barker, *A Mediterranean Valley: Landscape Archaeology and Annales History in the Biferno Valley,* Leicester, Leicester University Press: 254-87.

————, Barker, G. & Wade, K. (1980) 'Excavations at D85 (Santa Maria in Civita): an early medieval hilltop settlement in Molise', *Papers of the British School at Rome* 48: 70-124.

————, Gibson, S. & Mitchell, J. (1997) 'The making of a monastic city: the architecture of San Vincenzo al Volturno in the ninth century', *Papers of the British School at Rome* 65: 233-86.

Hoskins, W.G. (1955) *The Making of the English Landscape,* London, Hodder & Stoughton.

Hubert, E. (ed.) (1995) *Une région frontalière au moyen âge. Les vallées du Turano et du Salto entre Sabine et Abruzzes,* Rome, École Française de Rome.

———— (2000) 'Introduction', in E. Hubert (ed.) *Une région frontalière au moyen âge,* Rome, École Française de Rome: 1-25.

Jones, A.H.M. (1964) *The Later Roman Empire: A Social, Economic and Administrative Survey,* Oxford, Basil Blackwell.

Kurze, W. (1973), *I reperti d'argento di Galognano come fonti di storia,* in O.v. Hessen, W. Kurze & C.A. Mastrelli, *Il tesoro ecclesiastico di Galognano,* Florence, Centro per lo studio delle civiltà barbariche in Italia: 3-48.

La Rocca, C. (1998) 'La trasformazione del territorio in Occidente', in *Morfologie sociali e culturali in Europa fra tarda antichita e alto medioevo,* Settimane di Studio del Centro Italiano di Studi sull'Alto Medioevo XLV, Spoleto: 257-90.

Le Goff, J. (1988) 'The wilderness in the medieval West', in J. Le Goff, *The Medieval Imagination,* Chicago, Chicago University Press: 47-59.

Liebeschuetz, J.H.W.G. (2001) 'The uses and abuses of the concept of "decline" in later Roman history, or was Gibbon politically incorrect?' in L. Lavan (ed.) *Recent Research in Late-Antique Urbanism,* Portsmouth, Journal of Roman Archaeology Supplementary Series no 42: 233-45.

Llewellyn, P. (1986) 'The Popes and the constitution in the eighth century', *English History Review* 101: 42-67.

Bibliography

Lloyd, J. (1991) 'Farming the Highlands: Samnium and Arcadia in the Hellenistic and early Roman imperial periods', in G. Barker & J.A. Lloyd (eds) *Roman Landscapes: Archaeological Survey in the Mediterranean Region*, London, British School at Rome: 180-93.

—— (1995) 'Roman towns and territories', in G. Barker (ed.) *A Mediterranean Valley*, Leicester, Leicester University Press: 213-53.

Manacorda, D. (2001) *The Crypta Balbi: archeologia e storia di un paesaggio urbano*, Rome, Electa.

Mancassola, N. & Saggioro, F. (2000) 'Ricerche sul territorio tra tardoantico e altomedioevo: il caso di studio del Garda orientale', in G.P. Brogiolo (ed.), *Il congresso nazionale di archeologia medievale*, Florence, All'Insegna del Giglio: 127-31.

Martin, J.-M. (1980) 'Eléments préfeodaux dans les principautés de Bénévent et de Capoue (fin du VIIIe siècle – debut du XI siècle): modalités de privatisation du pouvoir', in *Structures féodales et féodalisme dans l'occident méditerranéen (Xe – XIIIe siècles)*, Rome, École Française de Rome: 553-86.

—— & Noyé, G. (1991) *La Capitanata nella storia del Mezzogiorno medievale*, Bari, Editrice tipografia.

Matthews, T.F. (1993) *The Clash of Gods*, Princeton, Princerton University Press.

Meneghini, R. & Santangeli Valenzani, R. (2001) 'La trasformazione del tessuto urbano tra V e IX secolo', in P. Delogu *et al.* (eds) *Roma dall' antichità al medioevo: archeologia e storia*, Milan, Electa: 20-33.

McCormick, M. (2001) *Origins of the European Economy*, Cambridge, Cambridge University Press.

Micheletto, E. (1998) 'Forme di insediamento tra V e XIII secolo: il contributo dell'archeologia', in L. Mercando & E. Micheletto (eds) *Archaeologia in Piemonte, III,* Turin, Allemandi: 51-80.

Molinari, A. (1994) 'Il popolamento rurale in Sicilia tra V e XIII secolo: alcuni spunti di riflessione, in R. Francovich & G. Noyé (eds) *La storia dell'altomedioevo italiano all luce dell'archeologia*, Florence, All'Insegna del Giglio: 299-332.

Moreland, J. (2001a) *Archaeology and Text*, London, Duckworth.

——. (2001b) *Casale San Donato*, unpublished manuscript submitted to the Ministero di Beni Culturali, Italy.

—— & Pluciennik, M. (1991) 'Excavations at Casale San Donato. Castel Nuovo di farfa (Ri) 1990', *Archeologia Medievale* XVIII: 477-90.

—— *et al.* (1993) 'Excavations at Casale San Donato, Castelnuovo di Farfa (Ri), Lazio, 1992', *Archeologia Medievale* XX: 185-228.

Negro Ponzi Mancini, M.M. (ed.) (1999) *San Michele di Trino (VC). Dal villaggio romano al castello medievale,* Florence, All'Insegna del Giglio.

Bibliography

Ortalli, J. *et al.* (eds) (2000) *Antiche genti di pianura. Tra Reno e Lavino: ricerche archaeologiche a Calderara di Reno,* Florence, All'Insegna del Giglio.

Paroli, L. (ed.) (1997a) *L'Italia centro-settentrionale in età longobarda. Atti del Convegno, Ascoli Piceno,* Firenze, All'Insegna del Giglio.

—— (1997b) *La Necropoli di Castel Trosino: un laboratorio archeologico pert lo studio dell'età longobarda,* in L. Paroli (ed.) *L'Italia centro settentriondale in età longobarda,* Florence, All'Insegna del Giglio: 91-112.

Patterson, H. (2001) 'The Pottery', in J. Mitchell & I.L. Hansen (eds) *San Vincenzo al Volturno 3: The Finds from the 1980-86 Excavations,* Spoleto, Centro Italiano di Studi sull'Alto Medioevo: 297-322.

Patterson, J. (1991) 'Villae or vici?' Introduction to section V, in G. Barker & J.A. Lloyd (eds) *Roman Landscapes: Archaeological Survey in the Mediterranean Region,* London, British School at Rome: 177-9.

Périn, P. (1992) 'La part du haut moyen âge dans la genèse des terroirs de la France médiévale', in M. Parisse (ed.) *Le Roi de France et son royaume autour de l'an mil,* Paris: 227-31.

Potter, T.W. (1975) 'Recenti ricerche in Etruria Meridionale: problemi della transizione dal tardoantico all'altomedioevo', *Archeologia Medievale* II: 215-36.

—— (1978) 'Population hiatus and continuity: the case of the south Etruria survey, in H. Mc Blake, T.W. Potter & D.B. Whitehouse (eds) *Papers in Italian Archaeology I,* Oxford, BAR Supplementary Series 41: 99-116.

—— (1979) *The Changing Landscape of South Etruria,* London, Paul Elek.

—— (1987) *Roman Italy,* London, British Museum Press.

—— & King, A.C. (1997) *Excavations at Mola di Monte Gelato. A Roman and Medieval Settlement in South Etruria,* London, British School at Rome.

Provero, L. (1998) *L'Italia dei Poteri Locali. Secoli X – XII,* Roma, Carocci.

Quirós Castillo, J.A. (1999) *El incastellamento en el territorio de la ciudad de Luca (Toscana).* Oxford, BAR International Series 811.

——, Gobbato, S., Giovannetti, L. & Sorrentino, C. (2000) 'Storia e archeologia del castello di Gorfigliano (Minucciano, Lucca): campagna 1999', *Archeologia Medievale* XXVII: 147-76.

Reynolds, S. (1994) *Fiefs and Vassals,* Oxford, Clarendon Press.

Ripoll, G. & Arce, J. (2000) 'The transformation and end of Roman *villae* in the West', in G.P. Brogiolo, N. Gauthier & N. Christie (eds), *Towns and their Territories between Late Antiquity and the Early Middle Ages,* Leiden, Brill: 63-114.

Bibliography

Roffia, E. (1997) (ed.) *Ville romane sul lago di Garda,* Brescia, Società Archeologica Padana.

Rupp, C. (1997) 'La necropoli longobarda di Nocera Umbra: una sintesi', in L. Paroli (ed.) *L'Italia centro settentrionale in età longobarda,* Florence, All'Insegna del Giglio: 167-84.

Sena Chiesa, G., Lavizzari Pedrazzini, M.P. (eds) (1985) *Angera Romana: scavi nella necropoli 1970-1979,* Rome, Giorgio Bretschneider.

Sergi, G. (1993) 'Villaggi e curtes come basi economico-territoriali per lo sviluppo del banno', in G. Sergi (ed.) *Curtis e Signoria Rurale interferenze fra due strutture medievali,* Turin, Scriptorium: 7-24.

Small, A.M. & Buck, R.J. (1994) *The Excavations of San Giovanni di Ruoti,* vol. 1: *The Villas and their Environment,* Toronto, University of Toronto Press.

Staffa, A.R. (1994) (ed.) *Lanciano e il suo territorio fra preistoria ed altomedioevo,* Lanciano, Comune di Lanciano.

——— (1997), 'I Longobardi in Abruzzo (secc. VI-VII)', in L. Paroli (ed.) *L'Italia centro-settentrionale in età longobarda, Atti del Convegno Ascoli Piceno,* Firenze, All'Insegna del Giglio: 113-65.

——— (2000) 'Le campagne Abruzzesi fra tarda antichità ed altomedioevo (secc. IV-XII)', *Archeologia Medievale* XXVII: 47-99.

Steuer, H. (1989) 'Archaeology and history: proposals on the social structure of the Merovingian kingdom', in K. Randsborg (ed.) *The Birth of Europe,* Rome, Danish Institute in Rome: 100-22.

Theuws, F. (2001) 'Maastricht as a centre of power in the early Middle Ages', in M. de Jong & F. Theuws (eds) *Topographies of Power in the Early Middle Ages,* Leiden, Brill: 155-216.

Toubert, P. (1973) *Les structures du Latium médiéval. Le Latium méridional et la Sabine de Xie siècle à la fin du XIIe siècle,* Rome, École Française de Rome.

——— (1983) 'Il sistema curtense: la produzione e lo scambio interno in Italia nei secoli VIII, IX e X', in R. Romano & U. Tucci (eds) *Storia d'Italia. Annali VI. Economia naturale, economia monetaria,* Turin, Einaudi: 3-63.

——— (1984) 'Conclusions', in Comba & Settia (1984): 403-7.

——— (1988) 'Intervento sulla relazione di Francovich-Hodges', in Francovich & Milanese (1988): 45-6.

——— (1995) 'I destini di un tema storiografico: "castelli" e popolamento nell' Italia medievale', in P. Toubert, *Dalla Terra ai Castelli,* Turin, Einaudi: 24-43.

Valenti, M. (1996a) *Poggio Imperiale a Poggibonsi (Siena). Dal villaggio di canpanne al castello di pietra,* Florence, All'Insegna del Giglio.

——— (1996b) 'La Toscana tra VI-IX secolo. Città e campagna tra fine dell'età tardoantica ed altomedioevo', in G.P. Brogiolo (ed.), *La fine delle ville romane: trasformazioni nelle campagne tra tarda an-*

tichità e alto medioevo (Gardone Riviera 1995), Mantua, Società Archeologica Padana: 81-106.

Van der Veen, M. (1985) 'An early medieval hilltop settlement in Molise: the plant remains from D85', *Papers of the British School at Rome* 53: 211-24.

Vera, D. (1995) 'Dalla "villa perfeta" alla villa di Palladio', Part 1, *Athenaeum* 83/1: 189-211; Part 2, *Athenaeum* 83/2: 331-56.

Volpe, G. (ed.) (1998) *La villa, le ecclesiae. Primi risultati dagli scavi nel sito rurale di San Giusto (Lucera): 1995-1997*, Bari, Edipuglia.

Ward-Perkins, B. (1997) Continuists, catastrophists, and the towns of Post-Roman Northern Italy, *Papers of the British School at Rome* 65: 157-76.

—— (2001) 'Specialisation, trade, and prosperity: an overview of the economy of the Late Antique Eastern Mediterranean', in S. Kingsley & M. Decker (eds) *Economy and Exchange in the East Mediterranean during Late Antiquity,* Oxford, Oxbow Books: 167-78.

Ward-Perkins, J. (1962) 'Etruscan towns. Roman roads and medieval villages: the historical geography of southern Etruria', *Geographical Journal* 128: 389-405.

Wickham, C. (1979) 'Historical and topographical notes on early medieval South Etruria', *Papers of the British School at Rome* 47: 132-79.

—— (1981) *Early Medieval Italy*, London, Macmillan.

—— (1984) *Il problema dell'Incastellamento nell'Italia Centrale: l'esempio di San Vincenzo al Volturno*, Florence, All' Insegna del Giglio.

—— (1989) 'Italy and the Early Middle Ages', in K. Randsborg (ed.) *The Birth of Europe*, Rome, Danish Institute in Rome: 140-51.

—— (1995) *Gossip and Resistance Among the Medieval Peasantry*, Birmingham, School of History, University of Birmingham.

—— (1997) 'Debate. The Feudal revolution IV', *Past and Present* 155: 196-208.

—— (1999) 'Early medieval archaeology in Italy: the last twenty years', *Archeologia Medievale* XXVI: 7-20.

—— (2000) 'Le forme del feudalismo', in 'Il feudalesimo nell'alto medioevo', *Settimane di Studio del Centro Italiano di Studi sull' Alto Medioevo* (Spoleto) XLVII: 15-51.

—— (2001) 'Medieval studies and the British School at Rome', *Papers of the British School at Rome* 59: 35-48.

Wolf, E.R. (1982) *Europe and the People without History*, Berkeley, University of California Press.

Zadora-Rio, E. (1995) 'Le village des historiens et le village des archéologues', in E. Mornet (ed.) *Campagnes Médiévales: L'homme et son espace. Études offertes à Robert Fossier*, Paris, Publications de la Sorbonne: 145-53.

Index

Index